In
Sickness
and
In
Health

A Husband's Story of Caring for a Mentally Ill Wife

Stephen Zehr

WESTBOW
PRESS®
A DIVISION OF THOMAS NELSON
& ZONDERVAN

WestBow Press books may be ordered through booksellers or by contacting:

WestBow Press
A Division of Thomas Nelson & Zondervan
1663 Liberty Drive
Bloomington, IN 47403
www.westbowpress.com
844-714-3454

ISBN: 978-1-6642-1505-4 (sc)
ISBN: 978-1-6642-1506-1 (hc)
ISBN: 978-1-6642-1504-7 (e)

Library of Congress Control Number: 2020924154

Print information available on the last page.

WestBow Press rev. date: 12/21/2020

Contents

FOREWORD

HUMAN RELATIONSHIPS ARE DIFFICULT EVEN IN THE BEST OF TIMES, BUT HAVING been a Marriage, Family and Child Therapist for 35 years, I have seen that mental health issues add a profound and pervasive dimension to the entire family dynamic. The book, *In Sickness and in Heath,* is the transparent struggle of a husband trying to keep his family together while they both deal with her mental illness. His candor and openness helps the reader not only understand the situation but also the agonizing feelings that accompany their struggle. Not only did I learn even more of their sufferings from the book but I often experienced it with them as I was a friend to both Susie and Steve for 20 years. My purpose as a friend and as a Christian therapist is to always point people to Christ, and we always see Steve innately going back to Jesus, seeking His mind and heart so that he can keep persevering and loving her well.

In Sickness and in Health we see God's hand and provision each day and in each struggle. Steve's acknowledgement of God's perfect plan for their lives allowed him to grow in a way he could have never imagined. God used their marriage to make him the man he is today. I really feel that everyone could benefit with the lessons found in the book *In Sickness and in Health.* You will be comforted to realize you are not alone in your struggles, but even more importantly that you have a loving Father who is always there with you and wastes nothing but uses everything for eventual good.

Terri A. Hands M.F.C.C., L.M.F.T.

PREFACE

As we go through life, few of us consider documenting our thoughts, authoring a book, and sharing it with the world. This is particularly true if sharing our story requires frankness about sensitive topics and public acknowledgment of our personal struggles. I am no different than anyone else in that regard except that in this case I truly felt a divine nudge to share this story. While it is difficult to be vulnerable and honest, this work is truly an exercise in trusting God.

Nearly fifteen years prior to writing this book, I felt nudged by the Spirit to share all that my wife, Susan, and I had been going through. I am not a natural writer, and a task like this can feel overwhelming to someone like myself. Nonetheless, I began to share the idea with friends. One of those friends had just felt nudged by the Spirit herself the night before that she, being a writer, was to help someone she knew to formulate and write a book. We both felt that was confirmation, or at least odd, and took mental note of it. We did not, however, pursue the project for various reasons. I put the idea on the shelf but never forgot about it.

Fifteen years later, and a year after Susan had passed away, I was at a reunion in Denver, Colorado, of some friends I had traveled the country with forty years prior. At that reunion, we went around in a circle, and each told our stories of what had been happening over the previous forty years. It was a heartfelt time of reconnecting and hearing of God's faithfulness through difficult times in life as well as joys.

That night, as I slept, I had a dream (I dream a lot) of writing a book about the story of my life with Susan. When I woke up, I prayed to the Lord about this reminder from fifteen years prior. Not unlike Gideon of the Old Testament, I expressed to God my hesitancy to plunge into a project of this magnitude and how I needed to put out a fleece to confirm His direction. I told Him, as if He didn't already know, that I am not a writer, and if I were hearing Him correctly to write this book, I would need some clear confirmation. When I finished praying, I opened a devotional I had been reading by Henri Nouwen to the place where I left off the day before. This day he was speaking to the need for all of us to tell our stories so that the world could be blessed by them and see God's hand in our lives. This was all the confirmation I needed. When I returned home to Minnesota, I began writing what you are about to read today.

I am not, nor do I claim to be, an expert on mental health or how to deal with a family member or friend who struggles with mental health. This is *my* story of how I believe God directed, sustained, strengthened, and supplied for me over a period of approximately twenty-eight years. Mental health has had many stigmas over the years, with most people not understanding it or knowing how to help others who struggle with it. It was particularly difficult in the '80s and '90s when Susan and I went through the pains of getting help and treating her disorders. I pray this book will, in a small way, bring you a sense of what it is like and dispel any fears and anxiety about people who struggle in this way. Most of us want to help but have no idea how, and so we end up staying clear of the issue. I hope my story can bring a sense of normalcy to what you or a loved one may be going through and encourage you to seek help in the Lord as well as in trusted friends and professionals.

INTRODUCTION

AT THE AGE OF TWENTY-FIVE AND ENGAGED TO BE MARRIED TO A BEAUTIFUL redheaded actress and model, I felt I had the world ahead of me full of hope and happiness. In many ways it is a good thing that we all go into life's biggest milestones without a crystal ball that shows us the future. If we knew what challenges lie ahead of us, we may never make the valuable choices to get married, have children, or start a business. Fortunately, we go into making those big decisions a bit blind and thus dive in and deal with life's challenges as they come, bringing some of the greatest joys that life has to offer. It's in those difficulties that we learn some of the most important lessons in life and build the most valuable relationships lasting us into eternity.

This is the story of my life with a dynamic and talented woman who, after several years of marriage, began to deal with an illness that would take us both down a long and difficult path together. As part of our marriage vows on May 28, 1982, we made a promise to one another to be together *in sickness and in health*. Of course, we meant those words, but I never imagined that promise would be as tested and tried as it was over a period of nearly twenty-eight years.

This is not only a story of a man's promise being tested but more of a personal struggle with trusting a God who promised to "never leave us or forsake us." It seems so easy to testify to faith and trust in God when things are going fairly smoothly, with food on the table, a roof over our heads, and a wonderful family. It is different, however, when those challenges affect your health—and especially your mental health. At least when we deal with physical issues, they can be seen and diagnosed easily. Mental health is not nearly as easy. There are no blood tests or x-rays that can determine the ailment. It is not an exact science. It must be diagnosed through extensive therapy and conversations about difficult things. Even after a doctor determines what the neurological issue may be, we laymen must understand the best way to live with it day after day. Even finding the right cocktail of medications is a painstaking and long process as the patient deals with side effects and reactions. These mental struggles can be debilitating, leaving a life partner to pick up the slack in the everyday responsibilities of managing a family.

Throughout my marriage I was forced to take on the responsibilities of husband, father, breadwinner, worship leader, and caretaker. Never had I been so stretched in my time and personal health but more importantly in my faith and dependence on God. At times, the burden simply seemed more than I could handle. Raising two daughters and caring for a wife with severe mental illness brought me to a breaking point many times. I was simply not a good enough man to love her as she needed to be loved. But God demonstrated His incredible faithfulness and strength to me over and over, day after day, month after month, year after year. No one can ever convince me that God is not a personal God who is aware of our weaknesses and pain and is ready at any time to bring comfort and strength when it is needed most.

It is my prayer that as you read this book it will become clear to you that this is not only a story of my caring for a wife with mental illness but of a faithful God who is there for each of us in our greatest time of need. He never promised to save us from life struggles. After all, we live in a war zone while on this earth between the powers of darkness and those of light. But God has promised that we would never go through any of it alone. His Spirit lives within us to guide, nurture, strengthen, and empower us with all that we need to not only bear the struggles but come out in the end with a stronger faith and reliance on the one who made us, knows us, and loves us beyond measure.

CHAPTER ONE

The Intensive Care Unit

(March 2018)

ONLY EIGHTEEN DAYS PRIOR, SUSIE HAD SEEMED PERFECTLY FINE. NOW, AS I SAT beside her in the ICU, it became clear that her situation—our situation—was turning quite dire.

As the doctor shared her prognosis and next steps, my incredible sense of fear was replaced with one of disbelief. Of all the struggles we had endured—years of treatments and tests—we'd always persevered. Through every challenge, every peak and valley, we'd leaned on God; He'd interceded, and we'd adapted to outlast every one.

So now what began as a seemingly simple cough had spun out of control. In a matter of weeks everything had fallen apart, and it all seemed so incredibly unfair. I was suddenly confronted with the bitter reality that this may be the beginning of the end—and, frankly, I wasn't ready.

Only days ago, she had been having difficulty breathing with a deep cough that left us both a bit concerned. Susie had suffered two separate bouts of pneumonia in the past, and we were always watching it closely for any return of the serious condition. We went to the doctor and had tests and x-rays taken to ward off any bronchiole problems. She was given an antibiotic, but as no pneumonia or even bronchitis was discovered, she was sent home for rest. The breathing difficulty and coughing, however, only got worse and culminated in much more concerning symptoms in a couple days. She was getting very weak and unable to bathe herself or even walk to the bathroom. It was clear this had advanced beyond what my daughter and I could do to nurse her back to health. After an ambulance ride to the emergency room, she was soon diagnosed with pneumonia and admitted to the hospital. The doctors said they did not know why the pneumonia had not shown up in the x-ray just two days before. They even brought out the x-ray to show me the difference in pictures. It was obvious to even me that her illness came on her very quickly.

I went to visit her in the hospital room the next day. She smiled as I entered the room. She was so happy to see me. I remember this specifically because over the past year she had become almost void of emotional expression due to all the medication she was on. It was so special to me that she showed actual pleasure seeing me as I visited her in the hospital. She was preparing to eat her evening meal and wanted me to join her. As I sat with her, it became clear that she was struggling to feed herself; with every bite, her hands shook uncontrollably. I didn't understand what the shaking had to do with pneumonia but assumed the doctors knew. It was heart-wrenching for me to watch her struggle, but I stayed with her and helped her finish her meal. My time was relatively short with her that night, as I needed to get some dinner myself and some well-deserved rest.

The next day I received an early morning call from a nurse at the hospital that Susie had difficulty through the night, and they needed to move her to ICU and intubate her to help her breath. This is the dreaded machine that Susie had always hoped she would never have to be put on—a tube would go down her throat into her lungs, and it was connected to a device that regulated her breathing since she was not able to do it on her own. I just looked at her wondering how this could be happening. She seemed fine only a week ago.

I immediately pointed out to the nurses that she was on some strong medications for her mental health and anxiety, and if she didn't stay on these medications, she would have some very serious symptoms show themselves and cause her to be unable to fight. They understood and reassured me that they would continue to give her those medications intravenously. I called my oldest daughter, Heather, who lived in town, and she came to visit often over the days to come as did many friends.

They tried several times to take her off the ventilator, but her anxiety would increase, and we would struggle to help her calm down. We would sing to her, rub her feet and hair, joke with her, and do whatever we could to get her to calm down and breathe on her own. Each time we tried, however, she could only last a day or two or even a few hours before needing to go back into a medically induced coma so she could relax and breathe. Susie had an advanced directive not to be put on any type of devices or external machines to keep her alive if it meant living without any quality of life. In fact, this—needing to stay on this type of machine—had been a pronounced fear in her thoughts and mind for many years. Because of that, when the doctors would try to extubate her, she would panic and even get angry with me. At one point, as I was trying to explain to her that this was only temporary, and she would be off it soon, she grabbed my arm and said, "It's my body." I knew she did not want to go on living if it meant being on a respirator, but I still had hope that she would come out of this and that the respirator was only temporary. It was an incredibly difficult place to be emotionally. I loved her very much and did not want her to be in pain or suffer in any way. I knew she did not want to have her death prolonged, but I did not want to give up hope of keeping her around either. Hearing her say those words to me was very painful because I only wanted to do what was best for her and ease her pain. That was the story of most of our marriage. I wanted so much to make her happy. I had no idea when we got together that life would be such a struggle for her and me as her husband—the person who loved her more than any other in the world. We had started our life together so differently.

CHAPTER TWO

—————————— ✣ ——————————

Our Meeting and Engagement

IT WAS 1979, AND I WAS ON A PLANE HEADING FOR FLORIDA TO BEGIN A NEW CAREER where I would be known as *The People Mover*. I had traveled the country with the singing group Cavalcade for a year and a half and lived a short time in both the Twin Cities, Minnesota, and Arlington, Virginia. I was now about to embark on a new adventure performing for elementary school children using singing, storytelling, and magic tricks to communicate the values of caring, sharing, kindness, and self-worth. I had been flown to Los Angeles, California, to train for a month and now was ready to begin my career as a performer—my dream come true. I was excited not to have to supplement my income by waiting on tables anymore!

After getting settled in my new home state of Florida, I began looking for a church. I had become more committed in my relationship with Christ and wanted to continue growing in my faith in a spiritual community. Through a friend, I found out about a small Christian church that met in a home. This group was made up of people who had become disillusioned by the organized church but still wanted to follow Jesus and be in spiritual community with others. This was a rather colorful group

of people with whom I felt at home right away. I soon made many friendships that have lasted to this day. In the group were five other individuals besides me who were artists or performing artists, and we quickly connected not only in our faith but also in our interest of the arts. Among this group was a tall, beautiful, redheaded model and actress named Susan.

Susie was a person you would consider the life of the party. She had an outrageous sense of humor, a joy, and an energy that were all charismatic and endearing. She had a childlike quality that I was drawn to which brought joy and humor wherever she went.

I was initially attracted to her talent as an actress and a beautiful dancer. She had appeared in many local and national television

commercials and had performed for a short time in Las Vegas as a dancer. She soon realized that she did not fit in at Vegas and moved back to her friends and support community in Miami/Fort Lauderdale, Florida. Susie was also a talented mime and

an all-around good performer, and she and I just enjoyed being together and even began to perform as a duo doing comedy sketches for friends and family. We did this for about two years before our relationship began to evolve from platonic to romantic. This was a bit of a challenge for me, however, because of the list I had formed in my mind of what a future wife might look like. Here was my shallow and carnal list of qualifications for my ideal mate:

1. shorter than myself, as I am only five feet six;
2. has dark or blonde hair (was not a fan of redheads);
3. comes from a Christian home;
4. enjoys but is not in the performing arts (so there would not be any competition);
5. is the same age or younger than me; and
6. is voluptuous (What can I say? I was not a beacon of virtue).

Susie did not actually meet any of these requirements. She was five foot ten; a redhead; came from a very troubled home with a single mom; was an actress, model, and dancer; was four years older than me; and while Susie had a beautiful figure, she was not necessarily buxom. I think what bothered me most, however, was her height. I was a very secure guy in many ways but always a bit self-conscious of my vertical stature. I remember calling my father about this subject because he was a short man as well, and his comment was, "Oh, I don't know about you, but I love a long pair of legs." Despite my dad's advice, I kept dragging my feet. It was clear that we were in love, enjoyed each other's company, and made each other laugh beyond what was normal for any couple. I was simply scared. One of my Cavalcade friends told me flat out that I better stop dragging my feet because Susie was at an age (twenty-eight) where she didn't want to date anymore, and I could lose her. Still, this was not enough for me to take the big step and ask her to be my wife.

Sometime shortly after those conversations with friends and family, I was driving down I-95 headed from Fort Lauderdale to Miami where Susie lived when I heard a very distinct voice. It was not like anything else I had experienced up until then. I knew right away it was the Lord speaking to me. Whether anyone else that would have been in the car at the time could have heard anything, I can't say, but I know I heard it clearly. The Lord was telling me that Susie was the one for me and to stop being afraid and ask her to marry me. I was so overwhelmed that I began to cry from the emotion of the moment and from the relief of the decision about Susie. As soon as I got to her apartment, I got down on one knee and asked her to marry me. It was not very romantic, as I had not planned this, and I didn't even have a ring, but I knew I had heard from God, and I wanted to act on that voice immediately. If I had to do it over again, I would have taken some time to plan out my proposal and make her feel incredibly special. This was the first of many mistakes I would make. She was thrilled, however, as I was, and we began a year of engagement culminating in our wedding on May 29, 1982. Since that time, I have often come to realize that God makes things abundantly clear on certain big decisions. He knows we need those stakes in the ground or Ebenezer stones to go back to, as things in the future could get very rough.

Chapter Three

&

Initial Concerns

THE FIRST FEW YEARS OF OUR MARRIAGE WERE NOT UNLIKE MOST OTHER COUPLES our age. We still had wonderful times laughing and performing together. We also landed jobs where we worked at the same company.

We made a lot of fun memories. We continued to perform together and were even asked to be the opening act for a concert with B. J. Thomas who was a well-known singer, famous for the song "Raindrops Keep Fallin' on My Head." We marveled at the opportunity and were so excited to perform before such a well-known artist. We continued to perform together and even called our duo *Steve & Susie Twogether*. (Notice the play on words?

No, it's not a typo) We performed for a variety of churches and condo associations. We were planning a show together much like *The People Mover* show except for middle-school students. We obtained some financing and began producing the show with recordings, costumes, and props. Halfway through the preparations, Susie felt we were on the wrong track and needed to stop working on the show and begin our marriage just working on us. I knew she was right about this, and we halted all work on the show. This proved to be such a wise decision, and I'm so glad she was listening to that inner voice and felt free to tell me her thoughts. It was obviously the Lord directing the both of us. We began to concentrate more on our relationship and life together. We, however, both brought our own baggage to the relationship, as well as our strengths, and it was a matter of understanding those strengths and weaknesses that provided our greatest initial challenges. Despite these initial struggles and adjustments, we were very much in love, and people said we fit together like a hand in a glove.

One of our biggest differences, however, was our family upbringing. I was raised in what appeared to her as the perfect home. I had a wonderful father and mother and an older brother and a younger sister. We went on family vacations, lived in the same city our whole lives, grew up with all the same friends, and basically, I had a great childhood. Susie, on the other hand, grew up with a single mom. Her mother had divorced her husband soon after Susie was born. Susie had virtually no relationship with her father. He worked all over the world and rarely ever came to see her. If he did, it was not for any length of time and basically communicated to Susie that she was not worth his time. She also knew from her mother that he never paid any child support and contributed nothing in any way to her upbringing. Her mother was an overworked single mother who we later found out struggled with mental illness. Her mother, Lorraine, had a bad case of OCD (obsessive compulsive disorder) at a time when no one had even heard of it before. Her mother had an extremely difficult life as a child. Lorraine had been put in an orphanage by her mother for a time because she felt she could not financially take care of her. This left Lorraine with a sense of abandonment and an inability to be loved. Not having a good example of motherhood to follow, plus struggling with mental illness, it is no surprise that Lorraine was not the best of mothers. When Susie was a child, there were times when her mother would wake her up at night and force her to take another shower because she had not gotten clean enough. Lorraine worked extremely hard to keep an exceptionally clean and, dare I say, sterile environment in her home. Because her mother worked full time, Susie had to go to her grandparents' house after school. There she would find herself in an environment totally opposite of her own home. Her grandparents rarely ever cleaned and even put new sheets on the bed over top of old ones to avoid having to wash dirty sheets. This is stark contrast to her home and brought little sense of normalcy to a little girl's life. Her grandparents completely ignored Susie, leaving her to entertain herself. In her mind she was on her own and felt like she was left to raise herself. She had no safe place, alternating her time between grandparents who ignored her while living in filth and a mother that yelled at her one moment and loved on her the next. We are now aware as well that Lorraine struggled with bipolar disorder. She would be pounding on Susie's bedroom door screaming at her at one moment and holding her and caressing her hair the next. Being raised without a safe space in her life left permanent scars that carried her into adulthood. Our childhood experiences could not have been any more different than they were.

Some of those differences began to show themselves in our marriage, and we dealt with them as they came up. One of the things that we soon realized was that Susie had some mental issues of which I was unaware, and some of them ran deeper than I understood.

Susie had an extreme fear of germs and dirt (OCD, like her mother) but I was under the impression that it was a mild case with her not wanting to get dirty. I was wrong. She had a fear of getting contaminated by ordinary things that most people would not even think about: bird droppings, public restrooms, walkways with hand railings … and the list went on. I was so proud, however, that she was aware of the lack of logic that went with her compulsions and how she wanted to overcome those fears. She even went so far as to take on a part-time job cleaning homes for extra income. For someone struggling with a fear of germs, I was amazed at her willingness to clean other people's homes and especially their bathrooms. She did this for only a short time, but when that job ended, she seemed to have her germ fears under control. We were both so pleased that it could be overcome by simply facing her fears head-on.

As you may have guessed, the struggles with OCD did not go away so easily. While she continued to battle with her contamination issues, she also began to deal with intrusive thoughts, which we later found out were a more intense form of OCD. These would be thoughts that would enter her head and attack anything that was important to her—primarily her faith in Jesus and in me. Susie held to the belief that while followers of Jesus could not be possessed by demons, they could certainly be bothered by them. She studied and listened to some teachings to that effect. Susie shared with me that when she felt these intrusive thoughts enter her mind, it bothered her a great deal. She asked if the two of us could pray for her to be delivered from these thoughts, which we both assumed were demonic. We prayed very passionately and intently and afterward felt better about the situation, although I never really felt that her struggle in this area went away. It did not seem to be frightening her as intensely so we didn't think much more about it. It did not go away, however, and in fact grew in intensity. We became so desperate for help that we contacted nationally and internationally known healers and spiritual leaders specializing in demonic possession. We continued to believe this was a spiritual problem because Susie had as a child messed around with a Ouija board with her mother. They had experienced some rather scary things that made them throw the board out, but Susie always thought she could have invited something into her mind and heart that would not go away. So, we continued to look for an answer to what we considered a demonic problem. If we had known then what we found out years later, we might have been able to address it more correctly at that time.

Another fear that was not so easy for Susie to overcome was her fear of having children. While I was aware of this before we were married, I naively thought that it would go away in time. This fear was not only rooted in the real physical pain she would endure in the birthing process, but also in the fact that she did not have a good role model to follow for motherhood. Her mother did the best she could at a time when mental illness was not usually treated or even recognized unless the person was unable to function in society. Susie was never allowed to use public facilities and rarely, if ever, allowed to go to a friend's house to play. As I said earlier, Lorraine would be sweet great kind to her and then suddenly, out of nowhere, break into a rage, calling her every name in the book, claiming she wished Susie had never been born. Her mother even went to the point of telling her how she had gone to an abortion clinic and was waiting for the doctor to see her but at the last minute, decided to keep her baby. She would tell Susie that she had made a mistake and should have gone through with it. I completely understood why Susie was petrified at the prospect of becoming like her mother.

After five years of marriage, I came to realize that her fear of motherhood might not go away, and I needed to resign myself to never becoming a father. I began to tell myself all the advantages there were to not having kids, like the financial security it could offer and the freedom to travel. I was trying to prepare myself for a childless fate, even though I had always wanted to have a wife and children and to build a family like the one I had experienced. I even remember telling God that I was willing to give up my dream of kids and would trust that He had a better future for me.

Very soon after my prayer, Susie came to me and said that God had clearly spoken to her and told her not to be afraid of childbirth or of her future as a mother. In only Susie style, she said. Okay. Take me! Let's have kids. We laughed about that for years because no sooner did we start trying than she became pregnant. We were so excited at her pregnancy that we announced it to all our friends right away, and they rejoiced with us. We were a bit premature in the announcement, however, as Susie had a miscarriage after five weeks of pregnancy. After a period of mourning, Susie became pregnant again, and we were excited—once again—looking forward to being parents.

Nine months later, on October 10, 1987, our first daughter was born. We named her Heather, not for any deep reason with great meaning, but simply because we liked the name and thought it was pretty. Heather had a more olive complication as a child, with dark hair and eyes resembling my side of the family. Susie's side of the family was more fair-skinned with hazel eye color. When she saw baby Heather for the first time, Susie's mother, Lorraine, said with a scowl and extremely unkind tone, "*It* doesn't look anything like us!" Susie was furious, as was I, and this escalated an already challenging relationship between Susie and me and Lorraine. Because of Heather's outgoing and loving personality as a child, however, Susie's mom soon came to have a strong and loving bond with her first granddaughter.

Our difficult times with Lorraine remained frequent and challenging. I remember that one evening when we had Lorraine over for dinner, she and Susie began an argument that got more and more intense to the point that Loraine started calling her daughter terrible names and degrading her in a way I simply could not tolerate. I told her she must stop or leave our home. Without saying a word but with a rather shocked look on her face, she got up and walked out. I had a hard time being with Lorraine, let alone loving her. At one point I became so frustrated I did not know what I was going to do. I asked the Lord to help me see her as He saw her so that I could love her as she needed to be loved. I was amazed how, after that prayer, I began to see the broken and damaged person she had become after a difficult childhood. When you can see a person the way God does, you begin to understand a bit more why they act the way they do. Our relationship did not improve dramatically for many years, but I eventually had her trust and love, and she commented how she even felt I understood her more than her own daughter. I believe that to be the sole result of God opening my eyes in answer to my prayer. Despite some improvement in our relationship with Lorraine over the years, we rarely allowed her to babysit because of our trust issues with her. Eventually, however, things got to a point where we felt we could leave her alone with our daughter on occasion.

We did not want Heather to be an only child, so we began to plan for our second. We had no difficulty getting pregnant again, planning to the very month when our second would be born. Katelynn was born on August 19, 1989. While Lorraine did not have the same initial negative reaction to Kate as she did to Heather, we soon began to notice, as the girls

grew and their personalities began to develop, that Heather had a much more outgoing personality than Kate. Lorraine soon began to show a great deal of favoritism to Heather over her sister. Kate was softer spoken and did not show as much affection to her grandmother and, Lorraine being the insecure person she was, did not respond well to her

reluctance to show a lot of physical tenderness. This infuriated both Susie and me. Katie was a beautifully tender and sweet child, however, that particularly loved her mother's attention. Susie loved it when Kate would cuddle close and just hang onto her mother. I think Kate was an answer to Susie's need to be needed and admired. She felt particularly close to her for many years. Maybe this was, once again, a part of Susie's childlike quality. She was always looking to be needed, loved, and validated, and those needs would often take precedence over her ability to take care of someone else and meet their needs.

Lorraine's preference for Heather became a sore spot for both Susie and me as well as for Kate, as she grew up feeling her grandmother

did not love her as much as her sister. When we brought this to Lorraine's attention, she, of course, denied it and was angry with us for even bringing it up. (This favoritism continued to be an issue until the day Lorraine passed away.)

Despite the tensions with

Lorraine, Susie and I and the girls had tremendous times together as a family. We took the children everywhere with us and involved them in many of the crazy performances that Susie and I did together. We had great times making typical family memories swimming in our friends' pools, trips to the beach, and just being crazy together. We continued to deal with the issue of Susie's mental health, however. She would go through serious bouts of depression but then also have extreme highs where she would do things in public that were funny but could be considered inappropriate. Her

behavior would occasionally embarrass her more reserved German husband at times, but I considered it all part of her zany personality that I also loved and embraced. She would dance down the grocery aisle pushing the girls in the cart, pretend to faint at the price of a prescription when picking it up at the pharmacy, pretend to be the Columbia Pictures Lady at the start of any of their movies in the theater, and do other off-the-wall things in public places. But we had a

great deal of fun being with Susie as well, and we took everything in stride. She was such a joy to be around, and she brought vitality to our lives. We even took five different family photos over the years that were unusual

but great fun for the entire family. These photo sessions involved my parents as well, as they helped stage and photograph them.

Susie continued to experience deeper bouts of depression and anxiety. Nothing I would do could make her happy, and she was enjoying our daughters less and less. We finally did seek some professional help for the depression that Susie was experiencing. Noticing Susie had a couple tics that were obvious to him, and after a lengthy conversation, the psychiatrist determined that Susie had a mild case of Tourette's syndrome. Having never heard of this before, we needed an explanation. He explained that the symptoms of Tourette's are often tics accompanied by vocalizations like sudden blurts or yelps or swear words. Susie, fortunately, did not show any of these verbal sounds, but she did have a sniff that accompanied every tic. I had grown so used to seeing and hearing this that I didn't think anything of it. This symptom, along with the extreme bouts of feeling depressed, made it clear to him that she was struggling with both Tourette's and depression. At that time, the only thing I knew about depression was when I felt low occasionally. I thought one could just put on a happy face and go on with your life, counting your blessings. The doctor told us that Susie's symptoms were due to a chemical imbalance in the brain and could be treated with a medication called Prozac. He wrote out the prescription, and we began our journey into the world of psychiatric drugs.

CHAPTER FOUR

God Was There

BEFORE I CONTINUE ANY FURTHER IN MY STORY, I MUST GIVE AN ACCOUNT OF an important spiritual experience I had that I believe prepared me for our future. While I was born in a wonderful Christian family and accepted the Lord at the young age of nine, I still went through many stages of growth and decline throughout adolescence and early adulthood, like most people I know. I was basically a good person who didn't rebel a great deal as a teen. Because I knew Jesus, I think down deep I felt like I deserved heaven, especially since I had, for the most part, stayed on the straight and narrow path.

I have heard of people experiencing a second blessing or baptism in the Holy Spirit, but I had never been through anything like that and was not looking for more than what I had in my relationship with Christ. I had been through individual mentoring both at a young age immediately following my conversion at nine years old and again as a young adult, not to mention the wonderful example my loving Christian parents gave me all through my life! I was going to church regularly, using my gifts in church, and had developed a wonderful community of Christian friends. I had everything I needed and was a shining example of a Christian man and husband and knew I was headed for heaven (he said sarcastically). While I was not perfect, I did have a strong work ethic, religious discipline both publicly and privately, and was just the kind of person God would welcome into His holy presence, right? The Lord, in His great love and wisdom, knew differently.

Susie and I were sitting at the dinner table one evening in 1985 listening to an a cappella group on the radio known as Glad. While we were finishing our meal, the group started to sing a song with the words to an old hymn called "And Can It Be," using a different melody. I had heard this hymn many times growing up in the church, but maybe because it was to a different tune or because it was done so beautifully, I was suddenly overwhelmed by what I understand now was the Holy Spirit. I felt this profound awareness of the sickness of my heart and depravity of my sin and of how much I did not deserve to stand in the presence of a Holy God. I began to weep, not only because I was taken aback by seeing myself as I really was, but also because of the joy I felt simultaneously as I was made aware of the incredible love and forgiveness of God to send His Son to pay for my sin. I cannot sufficiently describe how I felt with both the guilt and true self-awareness, while at the same time a peace and joy at the awareness of how loved and forgiven I was. I knew down deep that I did not deserve God's love and mercy, but He freely gave it to me out of tremendous love for me. I asked Susie if she felt anything happening, but she did not. This was a moment between God my Father and me. Even as I write this, it brings back tears as I recall God pouring out this awareness that I desperately needed but wasn't even seeking. My relationship with Christ grew exponentially, and I was able to pray and communicate with my heavenly Father in a way that was closer and more honest and real than I had ever experienced before that time.

I was committed to Christ and wanted whatever He had for me and my life with Susie. When we first got married, we were performing together in a live variety show that we performed in churches and some secular venues as well. After a few years of marriage, however, I began to feel like it was time for me to get more serious about life and go back to school to get my degree in music education. With this degree I would at least have the professional opportunity to teach music in grades K-12 and could add some financial stability to our household. During my school years, I worked at an athletic shoe store part time as well as a choir director at a small church about thirty minutes from our apartment. Susie took on a part-time job at a small boutique in a local mall as well as continuing to work as an actress in television. She had been doing this for many years and began to make a name for herself in the southeast Florida market in television commercials. Over the span of a few years, I quit the choir director job and took a position at a closer church as a youth director. It was not long before the pastor of the church saw that music was my greater gift, and I took on the responsibilities with the music of the church as well as the youth. Finding myself at this point in my life was a rather big surprise. As a young teen, I was sure I would become a star of stage and screen and had told my mother I never wanted to work in a church, which was her prayer. I guess her prayers won out, as I was now working nearly full time at a church, still working at the athletic shoe store, carrying a full load of classes in school, and singing in an operatic company. Susie was getting television work and was even cast in two episodes of a popular television series in the '80s called *Miami Vice*. All of this would sound like we were making plenty of money to meet our living requirements, but none of the jobs brought in much money, and we had no benefits. We were constantly looking to God to supply our needs.

God showed Himself close and real through many financial provisions that only strengthened our faith in Him. One of the gentlemen in our church was a multimillionaire and, along with his family, became good friends of ours. I was not aware of his wealth for a long time. Initially he had noticed me wearing an old blazer from high school and clothes for Sunday morning that were not the nicest. One day our pastor came up to me and said I needed to set aside a few hours that morning because he had a surprise for me. He then proceeded to tell me that one of the members of our congregation had wanted to bless me with some new clothes for Sunday mornings. I was surprised but excited to hear someone wanted to buy me a suit. As the day went on, I realized this was not just one suit but three suits, two blazers with three pairs of dress pants to match, shirts, ties, belts, and shoes to complete a full professional wardrobe. I was shocked! Then I found out that the same was to happen to Susie, as she would be getting several new dresses as well. These weren't bargain items either but rather high-end clothes that neither one of us had ever dreamed she would be able to wear. We were so touched and blessed. We soon found that they wanted to replace our old beat-up car with a beautiful car that they had owned. We again felt beyond grateful and could not believe the Lord had provided for us in this incredible way.

We invited them over to our place where we were living at the time for dinner to say thank you. We had a humble pot roast meal and showed them our two-bedroom apartment and told them we would be moving into our first house with some money that Susie's mother had given us for a down payment. We told them how excited we were and looked forward to having a yard and all the things people anticipate with their first house. The next day they pulled us aside to tell us they would like to completely furnish our new home. We were absolutely blown away by their generosity. I felt that it was just too much and that I should possibly not accept. I went to our pastor, who was a dear friend at the time, and asked his opinion as to whether I should accept their gift. I told him I knew that there was great value in a couple working together for their material possessions, and I did not want to miss out on what the Lord could want to do through that process. He reassured me that God would use other ways to teach us the lessons in life we needed to learn and urged us to accept their generous offer. We did, and $20,000 later had a house full of brand-new Ethan Allen and Thomasville furniture. This was indeed a supernatural gift from God.

I bring this up because I have come to realize over the years that when the path I'm about to go on is going to be intense and very difficult, God will often give me a supernatural experience to guide and sustain me through those difficult times.

CHAPTER FIVE

&

Pavillion

A FEW WEEKS AFTER WE SAW A PSYCHIATRIST FOR THE FIRST TIME FOR THE depression, and Susie began taking Prozac, we began to see incredible improvement over her moods. She had increased energy, and she began to seem really alive again. Susie was still Susie, though, with mood swings that would interrupt her days. She became creative again, after losing so much of that part of her personality, and started trying new things with passion and conviction. Believe it or not, one of those passions was for pet hamsters. She felt this compassion for disabled hamsters and began collecting these creatures that were blind or missing a limb. She bought an entire tube city for them and cared for them with great fervor.

She wanted to learn to play the drums, so we purchased an inexpensive set of drums for her to practice. I even had her play a couple times in church with us as she improved. This was a huge validation for her and made her feel so good about herself. Susie was always looking for something new to do that would prove that she was a worthwhile person with value. Unfortunately, nothing lasted long before she was onto another project such as writing, playing the harp, painting, and volunteering at the school or nursing home to validate herself. All these helped for a short time, but the responsibility of them became too much, and she would spiral down emotionally. She would get overwhelmed and feel it proved that she was the failure she believed she was.

After about a year on Prozac, Susie began to show signs of going back in the direction of depression, and we began to get concerned for her. Suddenly, everything took a dramatic turn downward, and she became very anxious and depressed once again, finding herself in bed for hours at a time during the day. She desperately wanted to get rid of all the hamsters and drop out of commitments she had made to others. She was making decisions without regard to their consequences, and once again we went back to the doctor to get help for her mental health.

Susie kept on experiencing deeper bouts of depression, anxiety and mood swings. Nothing I tried made her happy, and she once again was taking no joy from our daughters. The medications and side effects became so troubling to us that her psychiatrist recommended she go into a mental facility called Pavillion for a couple weeks to undergo some extensive counseling and to get medication management. I was completely shocked by this, because I have always been someone who just pushes through difficulties. I know I was not helpful in dealing with Susie's depression, as I could not understand why she was feeling this way and would advise her to just buck up. I tried my best to deal with everything, but I was totally inexperienced with depression or any mental illness, and at times when she just needed to cry or let out her emotions, I would try to *fix* it. I have since learned my lesson about how to be helpful to people struggling with these types of mental illness.

After Susie agreed to go into the facility, we conferred with a counselor friend of ours who offered to go with us to check her in. Susie was so incredibly frightened as she had to endure a strip search so the staff could take anything away from her that could be perceived as a danger to her or the other patients. This was so humiliating for her and made an already vulnerable person feel even weaker and smaller. When it came time for me to leave, she begged me not to go. As I walked away to go home, I will never forget her face as she looked at me as if to say, "I'm so scared. Don't leave me!" I just broke down sobbing in the car for the entire drive home. I was so glad I had my friend with me who was so supportive and kind.

I was told that I was not to come visit her for at least a few days, and her mother was *definitely* not to visit. I eventually understood the need to get her acclimated so she could get the help she needed, but it was difficult on her and me and our daughters to be separated for even a few days. Eventually, after what seemed like eternity but was only a week, I was able to go and visit but not allowed to take the girls with me. As I visited Susie in her room, she told me how much she hated it and didn't want to be there. Most of the other patients were dealing with substance abuse and could not relate to her, and some would even walk into her room at night and frighten her. Nonetheless, they required her to go to group sessions as well as craft and exercise classes. She also met with a special counselor and medical doctor to get comprehensive treatment. They started her on a regimen of medications to help the depression but also to help with her tics. After a week, they decided to release her on an outing to go home for a few hours to see her daughters and begin to acclimate to the idea of returning home. I was surprised that after a few hours at home with us, she was getting overly anxious again and wanted to go back to the hospital. This was a bit hurtful. I did not understand why being home would make her anxious. I had even updated our kitchen as a surprise for her by replacing the countertop and painting the cabinets because I knew it was something she wanted done, but even that did not get a smile out of her. The doctors told me it was a typical reaction because she was nervous about taking on any responsibilities again. They explained that she was living in an entirely stress-free environment with everything being taken care of for her, so it would be quite an adjustment for her to return to her normal life. We needed to give her another week before she would be ready to come home.

During the time Susie was in the hospital, I tried to be there as much as I could for Heather and Katelynn, who were six and four years old, while also doing my job. I have been a music director and worship leader of several churches since around 1985, and with that came a huge Christian community that were there to help us. I will forever be grateful for the people at our church who showed so much love and support to our family! They offered to babysit, clean our house, and make meals, and just be there for the girls and me. They were incredibly supportive of Susie as well. One friend who was a hairstylist even went to the hospital and cut and styled Susie's hair because he knew that would make her feel better. So many friends were there for our entire family, praying and counseling Susie and loving our girls. What a tremendous support the family of God showed to us at a time when no one really understood what was happening and my biological family lived many miles away in Illinois. They just loved us and were there for us. Even our next-door neighbors were so incredibly supportive, allowing the girls to swim in their pool, mowing our lawn, and helping in whatever way they could.

It was also during this time, as well as in many years to come, that I would find myself so frightened or frustrated that I would sit at the piano and play and sing out for help to God, and He would meet me there. Sometimes I would open the Bible and just sing a Psalm, or I would sing prayers through tears and anguish. These were very meaningful times, as the Lord was always there to meet me where I was. He promises to be there when we need Him, and He showed Himself to be so very real during my extreme times of loneliness and frustration. I've also come to realize how much music and worship in general can affect our outlook on life. The enemies of God hate to hear our praise and worship of God the Father and tend to flee at the sound of our singing. (Some of you may think people flee at the sound of your singing, but God loves to hear even a joyful noise if singing is not your gift) I will always hold these times alone with God very dear. They were a testimony to God's faithfulness and love.

After two weeks at Pavillion, Susie was finally allowed to come home. We began to ease her back into her normal routine. It took her some time to begin to take on responsibilities again, but after a while, she was able to be a mom and wife again. The adjusted medications proved to be highly effective and helped her to have a more positive outlook on life in general, and they gave her a great deal of energy. It was after this treatment of the OCD and depression that we began to see other symptoms show up as well as side effects from these powerful medications that would need to be treated in a different way. It all became extremely complicated not only to us but clearly even to the doctors we saw. One medication would be quite effective for treating the tics from the Tourette's syndrome yet would have a side effect that would agitate her anxiety issues. The medication for the anxiety would make her so sleepy that she would find herself in bed for way too many hours in a day, leading to even greater depression. It was a constant balancing act trying to find the right cocktail of medications that went on for many years.

During this entire time, I was trying so hard to balance being a husband, father, and breadwinner, and all this in somewhat of a glass house because of my position in the church. I was up front and visible to everyone as well as the girls and Susie. The first church I was at had a membership of around three hundred and later another church of nearly eighteen hundred. I'm sure this did not help Susie knowing that our lives were being seen by many people. This made me feel bad because I knew it added stress to her life, but it was what I did for a living, and God seemed to be blessing it. She was grateful for the help we received and the friendships it awarded us, but she did not always like the fact that everyone knew our business. I say that, yet Susie was the first one to tell people of our struggles. I think this was a hard balance for her as well. She was a very transparent person but didn't want anyone to be examining her Christianity and, in her view, judging her faith.

Susie always felt that she didn't fit into the whole "wife of a church staff person" thing. This became even more amplified when I was ordained in the Southern Baptist Church, and people started calling me pastor. She did not like the idea of being a pastor's wife. She liked some of the benefits that came with the position but did not like the pressure and responsibility that she felt came with it. This again showed me how her childlikeness became a detriment to her life. We all loved the humor and joy that she showed when she was feeling good, but she never seemed to be able to know the boundaries between acting with the joy of a child and taking the responsibilities of an adult seriously. I remember one time she thought she would play a joke on our pastor, who we did not really know that well, and myself. She wrote a note with the words *Help me. My husband is beating me* signed by her and placed it under the pastor's office door. She thought it was very funny, and everyone would get a good laugh out of it. Obviously, the pastor did not know whether to take it seriously or not. Fortunately, after a conversation with him, I was able to dispel any concerns he had. Unfortunately, this type of thing happened too often and was a constant source of embarrassment to me that she never understood. She also didn't understand why others did not find her jokes as funny as she did. In fact, behind her back and mine, they would call her crazy, not meaning it in an affectionate way. I knew, however, what some people thought of her, and it made me not only incredibly sad but furious at times. Many people simply have no understanding of what type of things people with mental health issues deal with. They can be judgmental and critical and make sure to stay clear of them. Others, rightly, feel compassion for them but do not know what to say or do, and so they stay clear of them as well. Both reactions can exasperate the person's feeling of self-worth. These people often find themselves more lonely and detached from others than most people. This was often the case with Susie, making those people that did reach out to her even more valuable.

CHAPTER SIX

An Overdose

THE MEDICATIONS SUSIE WAS ON WERE HELPING HER FUNCTION BETTER IN LIFE. She had more energy, and that gave her more productivity on her days. With the productivity came less depression and a much better outlook on her life with me and the girls. Unfortunately, with all these psychiatric medicines there are side effects that must be dealt with. She began to suffer from some of these including severe dry mouth, weight gain, more dramatic tics, and sometimes suicidal thoughts. Because she had been a model and an actress, the weight gain really bothered her. The dry mouth and tics were something she felt she could cope with but not the weight gain. Obviously, the suicidal thoughts were the greatest concern. We continued to go to the psychiatrist, and he would tweak the doses and types of drugs to find the best combinations that would work for her. We knew she needed them, but some seemed to be making things worse.

One day I came home from work and Susie told me she had taken an overdose of her tranquilizers to end her life. She was very frightened after the fact as she thought about leaving her daughters and told me about it. I called a friend to come and watch the girls (they fortunately did not know what had happened, as they were only around four and six) while I took her to the hospital. We went to the emergency room, where they gave her a charcoal mixture to drink to counter the effects of the tranquilizers. They also had her lie down on a gurney, and they strapped her wrists to the frame. This was frightening for both her and me. It was our first time experiencing this state requirement after a suicide attempt and was extremely upsetting. I had a friend from our church with me who had been lay counseling Susie, and she was very reassuring that this was necessary. The hospital staff told me that they would not release her unless I could reassure them that I was making an appointment to see another psychiatrist and that it was on the calendar. Of course, I did this, and after about twelve hours they released her to go home.

We found another psychiatrist, who started Susie on a relatively new medication that seemed to work very well with her system and proved to be one she would be on very many years to come. However, it seemed that some of the medications would work for a while but, as her body got used to them, would change in their effectiveness. I had to remember that she was dealing with Tourette's syndrome, clinical depression and severe OCD. Treating one disorder with proper medication would aggravate the other disorder, and it became rather complicated to figure out the right cocktail of medications with just the right balance of each. While one disorder would seem to move to the background under a medication, another disorder would become more prominent.

At one point, Susie began to experience even greater anxiety over her OCD. It would show itself in intensely evil thoughts, which became more upsetting than she could handle. It was not the fear of germs that was so debilitating but rather the terrible intrusive thoughts she would get. These were thoughts of blasphemy or cursing God, hurting herself or one of our daughters or myself with a knife, and other extremely upsetting thoughts that would just pop into her head. It is amazing to me as I reflect on those day that I never actually felt the girls or myself were in danger. She loved us all more than anything else in her life, and we knew that. Even when she was at her worst, I never felt we were in danger. We sought all sorts of counselors and spiritual healers in addition to the doctors. We were so desperate that we would look for help in some rather odd places. We consulted internationally known healers and nationally known therapists. Some would help temporarily, but we would still be back to square one eventually. We read books on all types of treatments that were not as mainstream. We went through so much money trying different vitamin supplements and organic healing methods as well as special tests.

After she had attempted to kill herself, it was always in my mind that this could happen again, so I was on a constant state of alert day and night. I would try hard to shield the girls from as much of it as I could. At times I would be successful and other times not. One day she would be perfectly fine and having great times with the girls, and other times I would be frightened to leave them alone with her as I went to work.

In my job, I would be preparing and leading worship services of praise to God. Even when I was not in a good place emotionally, I would need to do my job. At times, I felt hopeless, frightened, or even mad at God for allowing her to go through this and leaving me to deal with it. It was incredible, however, to see how God would use me on those days when I was at my worst. Inevitably it was on those mornings that people would come up to me and tell me how sweet the worship was that day and how it had ministered to them. I would thank them, shrug my shoulders, and say *thank you, God*, because I knew it did not come from me. The Lord made the scripture that says "In our weakness He is made strong" come to life.

Susie would often call me while I was at the church working and tell me I had to come home immediately because she was having another panic attack. At one point I was getting those calls three to four times each week. Thank the Lord we lived close to the church, so I could run home, calm her down, make sure the girls were okay, and head back to work. This would sometimes happen during the worship service as well. I remember one time especially. I was leading worship and noticed her get up and walk out. I knew the girls, being around four and six years old, were in either the nursery or Sunday school, so I did not let it worry me. When I finished leading, however, a friend led me to the office while the service continued and sat me down with the girls. They told me that Susie had left in our car crying hysterically and wouldn't tell them where she was going. I tried to get ahold of her by calling home (this was before cell phones), but there was no answer. I became extremely frightened at what she may be doing to herself. I imaged her driving herself into a tree or into a building or anything that would end her life. I remember holding the girls on my lap, and for the first time in front of them I was not able to hold back the tears. This, of course, frightened them, and they began to cry as well. We just prayed that God would keep her safe and that she would be found at home. After about thirty to forty-five minutes of what seemed like eternity, I was able to reach her at home. She had indeed considered harming herself but decided at the last minute to go home and go to bed. We all took a huge sigh of relief and thanked God for answering our prayer.

CHAPTER SEVEN

Our Daughters

ALL THE DRAMATIC EVENTS WITH SUSIE CAME SO FREQUENTLY THAT IT JUST became a part of our everyday life. I became quite worried about Heather and Kate growing up scarred in some way because of all the things they were facing with their mother. I would regularly pray not only for Susie to be healed but that the Lord would protect my daughters as well. As a father and husband, it would not be uncommon for me to be up through the night crying out to God for His help particularly regarding my innocent little girls. One of those nights I had a very vivid dream that I have held on to my entire life. I dreamed I was in wartime, and all the men were going off to fight in the battle. The women and children were being escorted off to caves where they would be kept safe during the war. I was very frightened to be separated from my children and was screaming out for them not to be taken from me. A woman in the dream who oversaw children's ministry at our church was taking them from me but trying to reassure me that they would be raised to love and fear the Lord. I kept screaming "No, no, you can't take my kids!" I woke up petrified in a cold sweat. Once again, as I had experienced before, I heard a clear, distinct voice telling me not to be afraid because His mercy and grace would cover them. I immediately felt an inexplicable peace come over me, and I was able to go back to sleep. I can say to this day that my two girls have both grown up to be very capable, kind, hardworking, understanding, and wonderful young women of whom I am enormously proud. I know God spoke to me that night and has been true to His word to me regarding their health.

I held on to that dream over the years through many different events. One such event was on another day when Susie was really struggling. We were all at home, but Susie was very agitated and crying and feeling hopeless. I could tell it was a day when she could not listen to anything that I would say to her, and she needed to take a tranquilizer and go to bed for a while. She would not do this, however, and once again decided to take the car, and end her life. She grabbed the keys to the car and headed for the garage. I tried and tried to stop her, even physically standing in her way but she was determined and was able to get past me and get into the driver's seat and lock the door. She began to back out of the garage and head to the main street. I was determined to stop her, so I jumped on the hood of the car and held on while she tried to get me off by driving more erratically. She only got out of the driveway and down the street a few yards before she stopped so that I would not get hurt. I was able to get the keys from her, calm her down, and get us both back into the house. Unfortunately, however, our daughters had seen that entire dramatic event. This was one of those times I claimed the dream God had given me to keep them from being scarred. While they were indeed frightened by this event and remember it vividly to this day, it did not leave any long-lasting problems in their minds, thank the Lord.

As the girls grew older, they needed to go to school. At first Susie and I had foolishly wanted them to be homeschooled because the schools in Florida, where we lived, were ranked forty-eighth out of the fifty states at the time. Of course, we soon came to our senses knowing there was no way Susie would be able to homeschool them, so we checked into enrolling them in a private Christian school that was in town where several friends taught. I knew that this was going to be a financial stretch for us and that it would mean many sacrifices in other areas. I was convinced it was necessary, particularly with the stresses at home that the girls were having to face.

They both began thriving at the school, but it was most definitely a financial burden. Again, the Lord provided in an incredible way. I secured a job as a part-time worship leader at the church that sponsored the school while also teaching band for their small ensemble. While I had been trained, I was not really qualified to teach band instruments, but they assured me they wanted me to lead this small group of students, so I took the position. After a year I again told them I was not qualified to develop the program they wanted, but I would love to teach chorus and drama if they wanted to develop a performing arts department. The headmaster was delighted at the prospect, and I took on those responsibilities.

All this teaching made it possible for my daughters to go to the school at a discounted rate. I was thrilled because it was the perfect place for them, and they had made many friends. Even with the discount, however, we were struggling so much to make ends meet. Medical expenses for Susie and living expenses, due to her inability to cook most meals, were climbing, and I was stressing out. I now had four sources of income as I balanced leading worship, teaching at the school, singing in an opera company, and doing television commercials plus cleaning and cooking and doing most of the work taking care of the girls. This is not to say Susie was in bed doing nothing all the time, but her ability to do anything consistently was practically nonexistent. She tried taking on extra jobs but could not stick with anything because of her mental health. I felt I was in overload as I tried to do it all. I was just about at a breaking point because of our financial situation when the headmaster of the school saw me walking down the hallway and started a casual conversation with me. He asked me how I was doing, and I told him that I was fine (I lied) but that our financial situation was a bit stressful. He then made a comment about the assumption that my girls were going to the school at no charge to my family. I explained that they were going at a discounted rate, but it was still a bit much for us. He immediately told me that from that moment on they would be going for free and that was no longer to be a concern for me. I thanked him, went to my car, and broke down crying at the relief of that pressure. God continued to show His love for us and to remind me that He knew of our struggles. It brings tears to my eyes even now as I write this. Over a period of ten years we saw God provide for us to the tune of about $180,000 including the inheritance that Susie got from her dad that she barely knew and the down payment for our house that Susie's mother was able to provide. God had been so incredibly good to us even through our battles with Susie's mental health.

CHAPTER EIGHT

A Sidetrack

AFTER ABOUT ELEVEN YEARS OF WORKING IN A CHURCH, I FELT GOD WAS leading me into another field of ministry. With the encouragement of a friend and future partner and much prayer, I decided to go into business editing fundraising videos for churches and other parachurch organizations. This was at a time when all video was done without the aid of computers. My partner and I felt we were getting in on the ground floor by using digital video editing, meaning everything was done on the computer. This was brand new technology, and many in the video industry were skeptical about it going digital. This proved to be a wonderful creative outlet for me but quite a financial burden once again. All of this also took place before I had that conversation with the headmaster allowing my daughters to go to the private school for free. I must have been nuts to do this but, being the adventurer and risk taker that I am, I began working from home now carrying business debt along with my partner. While it was a relatively short time in business, I can say I learned a lot.

One thing I learned from this adventure is that even if I hear God incorrectly, He is gracious and allows me to get off track but eventually steers me back to His ultimate will for me and my family. This financial stress left its mark long after I gave up the business because the debt remained, and Susie had an exceedingly difficult time dealing with it.

I had been working very hard at my different jobs to make ends meet, but the truth was that with the debt, medical bills (we now had no medical insurance as I had several part-time job but no benefits), and side expenses due to Susie's health, we were really struggling again. Susie had had one too many calls from creditors and felt she could not take anymore. She blamed all our problems on me, as she had done frequently, and decided to do something about it. She packed up, took the girls out of school, and drove to her more distant relatives in the Tampa, Florida, area. We were living in the Fort Lauderdale area, so it was about five hours away. The girls were twelve and ten by now and were very aware of the situations with Susie and did not like the idea of going with their mom to Tampa without me. They knew something was up, and Katie continually asked her mom where dad was and why wasn't he going with them. When I got home from work that day, I found a note on the counter telling me of her frustration and that she had left with the girls to Tampa. I was so upset. How could she do this to me when I was working so hard to support her and the family? I got in a car and drove the five hours to meet up with her at her cousin's house. When I got there, her relatives didn't really know what to do. They arranged for me to meet with a financial person to look at our situation and give any advice that might help. After meeting with him and explaining our entire situation, he felt I had been doing everything right to get out of our debt and was sympathetic to the struggles that I had dealing with Susie's mental illness. Some of her relatives were less kind and were angry at Susie for what she did to me and the girls. We both drove back home in our separate cars to return to our life. The girls did not know what had triggered that episode with their mother but were upset about it, and it remains a difficult memory.

As I alluded to earlier, looking back, I feel quite certain that the whole video business was not God's best plan for me, and I misheard Him. Hearing from God is not a science but a practiced communication skill that requires being open to Him and not allowing your own thoughts and wishes to get in the way. Obviously, I have not perfected this skill and have misheard God on several occasions. The beauty of a relationship with God is that He knows we are not perfect at it and allows us to make mistakes but always steers us back on the correct path. We really do not need to fear making a mistake because, like an earthly father, He loves us enough to bring us back in line with His will, where we find peace and joy.

CHAPTER NINE

A Serious Attempt

DURING THE TIME I WAS IN THE VIDEO BUSINESS, SUSIE HAD BEEN HAVING HER normal ups and downs. Some days she would be functioning in the normal way of any homemaker. She would be cleaning, cooking, taking care of the kids, picking them up at school, going on outings with them, and so forth. Other times, however, she was so depressed and distraught that she would be in bed for days at a time.

It was during one of her extreme down times that she again tried to overdose on her tranquilizers. This time was different, however, in that she took an extreme amount, and no one found her until it was dangerously late. When we did find her, we immediately called the ambulance, which took her to the hospital, where she was eventually admitted into ICU to try to get her vitals back to normal. This was very frightening for me and the girls. While I did get someone to watch Heather and Kate most of that time, they wanted to be with me at the hospital as well to be close to their mother. She ended up in the ICU for only two days, but it seemed like eternity. I will never forget a man who was in the ICU waiting room with me. He evidently was there for a relative of his, but when he found out that I worked at a church and after some conversation realized he had come to visit our church, he became rather aggressive. He told me of the sermon that was preached that Sunday and how the preacher had said that sometimes God allows illness and struggles in our lives to cause us to grow. He was very much in disagreement about that and felt that any illness was a lack of faith on the ill person's part or the family. I was in no mood to discuss that with him and was somewhat shocked at his lack of compassion and understating of our situation. It reminded me that sometimes we Christians can feel we have an answer to everything and without any kindness or compassion impart our *great wisdom* to hurting people. It was at that point I decided I never wanted to be that type of person. I wanted to put love and kindness ahead of whatever doctrinal concern I may have. "And now these three remain: faith, hope and love. But the greatest of these is love" (1 Corinthians 13:13 NIV).

As Susie began to improve and prepare to leave the ICU, her psychiatrist said that she needed to go to a mental facility and would not allow her to be released to my care. Because of our financial situation and the fact that I was between church jobs and did not have health insurance that covered mental health issues, she was taken to the county psychiatric facility. To hear Susie describe it, this hospital was akin to the hospital in the movie *One Flew Over the Cuckoo's Nest*. She described it as filthy and full of crazy and dangerous people, and she was extremely frightened. She begged me to get her out and take her home, but it was out of my hands. I could do nothing. If we had the money, I could have had her transferred to a private facility to get the treatment she needed, but that was out of our reach. Once again, our church family came to the rescue. They took up an offering and raised the money ($5,000) we needed to get her transferred. I will never be able to thank those people enough for the generosity and kindness they showed my family.

Susie's doctor said that her depression was too deep to effectively manage with medications alone, and he suggested she go through a series of ECT treatments (electroconvulsive therapy). I knew so little about all this stuff, and while I tried to learn quickly, I had to trust the doctor to know what was best for her. The only thing I knew about ECT was from the movies, and it was not good. In fact, I did not even realize they still performed that kind of treatment in the 1990s. The images that came to my mind were people being hooked up to electrodes and writhing on a table while their brains were shocked with intense amounts of electricity. The thought of Susie undergoing that kind of treatment sent chills down my spine. I wanted the best for her but wondered if this could possibly be the best thing for her at this point. I was forced to trust the experts, who said it was what she needed. She underwent a series of ECT in the hospital but would need to be released home and return to finish with outpatient treatments. I suppose if we had had the money she could have stayed for the entire round of treatment, but since we did not, I needed to carry the responsibility of caring for a patient who had just gone through this type of treatment. While the ECT did not incapacitate her, she was not very sharp afterward and required extra care.

I will never forget one visit that the girls and I and Susie's mother took to the hospital. We were in the waiting room, waiting for them to release Susie to come see us when the electricity went out for a short moment. We all looked at each other in silence in the partially dark waiting room. We were all wondering what had just happened. At that time, Susie's mother said in only a way that she could say in all seriousness, "Well, they must be treating another poor soul!" We all paused, looked at each other with blank stares, and then broke out in laughter at the absurdity of our presence at this hospital going through what we were. It felt so surreal. The laughter did ease some of the tension we were all feeling.

These treatments were indeed successful at shocking Susie's system out of the depression she was in, but we never knew if they left side effects on her memory. She always had issues with remembering things, but it seemed to increase after those treatments. We will never know for sure. I am grateful to God that ECT was available to us as a treatment because it was effective in breaking the cycle of depression that was spiraling downward. I know that this treatment does not always work for other patients and can leave long-lasting side effects. Thankfully, we were not one of those cases.

Unfortunately, that was not the last time that Susie attempted to take her life or threatened to do so. One time while I at was at work, and the girls, now thirteen and eleven, were at home alone with Susie, Heather heard her mother crying out for her from the master bedroom. Heather ran into the bedroom and then realized her mom was calling out from the master bathroom. She found her mother naked in the bathtub holding a knife and threatening to cut her wrists. Susie was crying hysterically. With all the maturity of an adult, Heather talked her down, took the knife from her, helped her get dressed, and laid her mother on her lap, stroking her hair to calm her down until she fell asleep. Heather acted, in many ways, like the mother in their relationship. After she calmed her mother down, she then went to attend to her younger sister who was, because of Heather, sheltered from the worst part of this and other situations. To this day I am amazed at how Heather was able to deal with not only this but so many other dramatic incidents that came along when I could not be there. God truly blessed this little girl with wisdom and maturity beyond her years.

CHAPTER TEN

Lorraine's Death and Moving On

SUSIE HAD ALWAYS PARTIALLY BLAMED ME FOR HER EMOTIONAL STRUGGLES, BUT most of that blame went to her mother. With the exception of Susie, the girls and me, Lorraine was all alone. She had no other family to speak of except for some rather distant relatives with whom she had burned some bridges after a bad monthlong trip with them around the country. As Lorraine aged and needed help, we were the ones to take on the burden.

At one time Lorraine had fallen in the bathtub at her apartment, which was not far away. She had been drinking and lost her balance in the tub. She had the water running and could not remember how to turn it off. I rushed over to her apartment and, with the extra key Susie had, went inside, covered her with a couple towels, turned off the water, and got her in her bed. We realized that she was not doing well living alone any longer, so we had to make some decisions. Rather than put her in a nursing home (she was far too young at that point), we went so far as to build a mother-in-law suite onto our house at Lorraine's expense, so she could stay close to us but be totally separate at the same time. It was a beautiful apartment with one bedroom, a small living room, a kitchenette, a full bath, a walk-in closet, a separate washer and dryer, a separate thermostat, and a separate entrance. We thought this would really make her happy. We were wrong!

Lorraine was in the habit of using some very colorful language, and she did not hold back when describing her new apartment. She also regularly complained about Susie's cooking, the way she was raising her daughters, the way she dressed, and basically anything Susie tried to do to please her. It did not help that Lorraine was an alcoholic, and we finally had to hide any liquor she purchased on her own. She was furious with us most of the time and made threats of many kinds to us. Once we even had to call the police on her for being verbally violent and threatening. We knew nothing would really come from that except to put some fear into her as to the way she would treat us. We were wrong, as it got her more riled up. Eventually, after about four years, we had to make the decision to put her in an assisted living facility. This was the first of the several places we found for her, all of which were worse than her apartment, in her opinion. In the third assisted living facility, her health took a turn for the worse, and she began to stop eating and eventually passed away. Even though Susie did not have a good relationship with her mom, she never stopped trying to get her love. At one point, Lorraine became so weak and struggled to talk so much that Susie thought maybe she was hanging on thinking she still had to take care of her daughter. Susie told her she need not worry about Susie's future. She reassured her that I was there to take care of her, and she could just let that go. Lorraine looked up at Susie and, using colorful language, exclaimed, "You think I am dying!" Of course, she was dying, but that is just an indication of the type of woman she was. Susie and I had several good laughs over that for many years.

Lorraine, for most of our marriage, was not happy with Susie's choice for a husband, either. I was not tall enough, wealthy enough, or the leading man type of guy seen in the movies. She and I had an unusual relationship in that she knew Susie needed someone like me to take care of her daughter. Because I was doing that as well as showing her some respect as Susie's mother, she began to warm up to me. At one point, however, I was finding it so difficult to deal with her that I just cried out to God to help me love this broken woman: to see her through the Lord's eyes. God granted that request, and I began to see her in a more compassionate and understanding way. She was still *very* difficult, but I seemed to be able to understand why she acted the way she did. I felt God had impressed on me that while I may not be able to respect Lorraine or anything she said, I *was* to respect her role or position as Susie's mother. We are commanded in Exodus 20:12 to "honor [our] father and mother." I could honor her while not truly respecting her opinions and advice, and that is what I tried hard to do. Near the end of Lorraine's life, she thanked me for showing her so much love, affection, and respect. She said that she even thought I loved her more than Susie did. Of course, that was not true, and I told her so. I told her Susie loved her very much. I am grateful that God gave me a heart for Lorraine that I truly was not able to have on my own.

Even though Lorraine had treated Susie so badly over the years, Susie still consistently prayed that Lorraine would not be alone when her time came to leave this earth. We had a pastor friend talk with her, and he reassured us that even though she was as troubled as she was, he really felt she understood and believed that Jesus was her savior. That gave a sense of peace as her time came to an end. God answered Susie's prayer, as she was able to be by her side as life left her body. After Lorraine passed away, we held a small memorial service in our home with about five other people besides our family in attendance. Our girls could not find much to say about Lorraine that was a fond memory, but we still wanted to respect the life she lived and the role she played as their grandmother and Susie's mother. I personally felt that the Lord used her in my life and taught me a great deal about how to love the unlovable. She was a difficult person but still loved by God and was a child of His. Susie felt she may finally be able to close an extremely difficult chapter in her life with the death of her mother. We all hoped to see some progress in her health as she could now stop hearing that reinforcement of negativity from Lorraine.

We wanted to have more family vacations together now that Susie's mother was gone, so we did just that. We took a trip to Key West, Cape Kennedy to see a shuttle launch, and Universal Studios. We also went to Marco Island one long weekend. At that time Susie was heavily medicated for all her issues and not operating at 100 percent. We rented a couple Jet Skis to ride in the ocean together. Susie was unable to get on the Jet Ski by herself and unable to get off without help. It was so clear to me and the girls that she was not herself, and it made us sad. This once very vibrant and adventurous woman was unable to do all that she normally loved. Once again in hindsight I think she was probably overmedicated at that time, but we were just trying to do the best we could and trusted the doctors.

We also decided to take our first real road trip to Illinois to visit my parents and brother and family. We packed up our new (used) Ford Explorer, which we had purchased with Susie's inheritance from her father, and started on the road. Right before we hit Tallahassee, Florida, the skies opened, and we found ourselves in a torrential downpour. Everyone started moving slower on the interstate. I slowed down as well but not enough. We began to hydroplane and spin around out of control off the road, smashing into a group of trees. We had never been in an accident big enough to cause the airbag to deploy until then. If you have been in an accident of that magnitude, you know the smell that comes from gas in the bags. I thought we were on fire. I yelled for everybody to get out of the car. We all piled out, finding our luggage had been thrown far from our vehicle on the side of the highway. I must have looked a sight because the girls acted scared as they looked at my bloody face from the airbag abrasions. An ambulance came and took us all to the local hospital, where we found that Susie had a broken collar bone. She was in a lot of pain. Fortunately, I had relatives that lived in Tallahassee, and they took us in for a few days to recover before making the rest of the trip. After all this was our first real road trip vacation, and we did not want to let the accident hold us up. The girls and I were fine after a couple days, but Susie was still in pain. I did not realize how much pain because she always seemed to be in pain over something. We decided to continue to Champaign, Illinois, where my parents lived. It was clear, however, when we got there that Susie was not going to be able to go any farther. We decided the girls and I would continue up to Chicago to visit my brother and then drive home to Florida on our own. Susie would stay with my folks and then fly home to Fort Lauderdale when we arrived back to pick her up at the airport. The girls and I had one of the best times together we ever had, although we all got nervous every time it rained. I think Susie enjoyed being nursed to health by my mother as well. She got to experience  what it was like to have a healthy person act as a mother to her as well as a present father figure in my dad.

Since Lorraine was the only immediate family Susie had in Florida, and all my family lived in the Midwest, we decided it may be time to leave Florida and move up north. I began looking for another church somewhere north of Florida. That could be just about anywhere. I found a church looking for a full-time worship director in Lakeville, Minnesota. When I saw the location, I remember saying to the Lord that we wanted to move up north but not to Siberia! I continued my search and sent out my resume to several other places, but that church in Lakeville continued to be at the forefront of my search. Finally, after a month I decided maybe the Lord had this place in mind for my family, and I sent out my resume. Soon after I sent it out, I got a call from them and within a relatively short time plans were made for us to move to Minnesota. This was an amazing act of God as well. My girls, now ages twelve and thirteen, were excited to leave and start a new adventure as well. When middle school girls looked forward to packing up and moving to an entirely different place at the expense of leaving their friends, I found that to be a sign from above.

We hired a moving company to pack up all our furniture, and we had planned on driving our two cars all the way up to Minnesota. I made this decision absentmindedly without considering Susie's anxiety issues. As we left Fort Lauderdale and headed north, our first stop was in Orlando. That night in the hotel I began to realize how incredibly difficult this was going to be for Susie to drive that many hours. From Fort Lauderdale to Orlando is about five hours, which made me extremely anxious about driving to Atlanta on our next leg of travel. When we got to Atlanta the next day, we hit the city during evening rush hour in a thunderstorm. Heather was riding with Susie the whole time trying to keep her mother calm without having much success. We would stop periodically while Susie calmed down and let a panic attack run its course. We also had our two dogs with us, which did not help the situation. In hindsight I should have had the car towed by the moving truck and us all drive together. As I have said before, I made so many mistakes.

The next day we planned to drive from Atlanta to Champaign, Illinois, where my parents lived. We started off on the trip but still found ourselves having to stop every few hours. I called my parents and told them I did not think Susie could make the entire drive and could they come and meet us about an hour south of Champaign to help us drive the remaining distance. They agreed and started out on their journey to meet up with us. The closer we got, the more I realized she was doing worse than even anticipated. I called my folks again and asked them to meet us in southern Illinois near the Kentucky border. Soon after that call, I had to ask them to come all the way into Kentucky. Eventually we did meet up with them in Paducah, Kentucky, where my mother took over driving our car, my dad driving their car, and me driving our second vehicle. We realized that Susie simply was not going to be able to drive anymore and that my folks were going to have to help us get up to Lakeville, Minnesota. We carpooled the rest of the way and finally made it safe and sound. It was an extremely trying time that I never want to relive again. It was particularly hard on my oldest daughter, Heather, as she had to try to be the calming force in her mother's life as she drove. This was far from the first time Heather was in this position of taking care of her mother. Maybe that is one reason Heather is such a nurturing and caring person to this day. That trip was frightening for all of us, but once again the Lord saw us through it.

CHAPTER ELEVEN

Here We Are, Minnesota

OUR FIRST YEAR IN MINNESOTA WAS ONE FILLED WITH A LOT OF NEW AND exciting things. Everything was an adventure for us as the girls saw their first snowfall, and we began to experience the friendliness of Minnesotans. We were welcomed with open arms by our new neighbors and our new church. Everything looked encouraging in our new life.

Susie was back to her fun and whimsical self, which is part of what caused me to fall in love with her in the first place. Our Minnesota house was on a hill with a steep driveway. The day the moving truck arrived it was parked at the end of our driveway with the door to their semitractor trailer open at the foot of the hill. Susie saw this as an opportunity to try something new and adventurous. She got on her bicycle and took off from the top of the

driveway attempting to ride into the tractor trailer. She obviously did not make it, as she fell off the bike, tumbling off the moving ramp and nearly breaking something. Fortunately, she made it through that unscathed but managed to break her ankle a few days later when she rode her bicycle full force through the woods, hitting a hole and falling hard to the ground. We got acquainted with the new local hospital right away as we took her to the emergency room. She ended up having a few rods surgically implanted to help her ankle bones grow back correctly. We were not yet on health insurance, as I was between employment, but were able to retroactively pay for Cobra and get ourselves covered.

Heather got adjusted to school as a ninth-grader fairly soon. In Lakeville they were still operating with a three-year junior high school, and so she was in the top class in her school. Also, because she was so outgoing and confident, she made friends right away with little adjustment period. Kate, however, struggled to fit in. She found herself being bullied and called names and was unhappy for almost a year. She was much more soft spoken and found herself not only dealing with the normal junior high school growing pains but also being the new kid in town. Fortunately, she met a dear friend from out new church and they became fast friends. They sat together at lunch and became close. After a very rough year with her crying every day before school, she eventually made new friends and felt right at home. Susie joined the choir at church and went to lunch with friends and overall felt a part of this new church family.

We had some wonderful times as a family as we went on new excursions to apple orchards in the fall, raking leaves (first time is fun), bonfires and s'mores, skiing in the winter, the winter carnival, making snowmen, fires in the fireplace, the joy of spring after a long, cold winter, and all of the wonderful summer festivals in Minnesota. We took several wonderful vacations together to New York City, where we saw a couple shows and the typical tourist attractions. We also went west to see Mount Rushmore and the Badlands of South Dakota. It was wonderful having Susie back to her old self, or at least functioning better, and enjoying her family and life in general. This did not last too terribly long, however, as she began to slip back into despair and frustration.

Susie began trying to find some part-time employment but struggled with any kind of consistency in her moods and mental health. She tried so hard over and over but continued to fall short of the minimum requirements of any of the jobs she tried. We began to realize that there was no way for her to ever work again other than sporadic temporary jobs. A friend recommended that we file for disability insurance since it was still financially difficult to meet her needs as well as everyday living expenses. Although it usually takes several times applying to the government to receive these benefits, we were able to receive them on our first try. I, once again, saw the Lord going before us and not only supplying our needs but making it easier than the process might otherwise have been. It was a tremendous help to us particularly since they paid retroactively over two years. It was an incredible blessing and act of provision from the Lord!

Susie began to show more and more signs of extreme anxiety and an inability to make decisions. It was not uncommon for her to call me, after leaving to go shopping, from a parking lot having a panic attack and unable to drive home. When I would arrive at the car, she would be sobbing uncontrollably, and it would take at least thirty minutes to calm her down to the point of driving home with me following close behind. The girls were feeling less and less comfortable riding in the car with her as her anxiety would affect her decision making while driving. At one time she was at a gas station preparing to fill the car with fuel. She got very confused at how to use the pump. She ended up opening the pump to release the gasoline *before* she had the nozzle in the tank. Gasoline went everywhere, and she panicked. The girls were frightened, and the station attendant came running out yelling at her wondering what she was doing. Her anxiety simply got in the way of making normal everyday decisions we all take for granted. At other times she would be so anxious that she would turn down the wrong side of the street, driving into oncoming traffic. At times she would simply get lost and call me to navigate her home. She was always a bit directionally challenged but became more and more uncertain of herself in general and particularly driving, even in town. It was clear that her driving would be limited to a few close trips from the house.

The girls, now in high school, were coming into their own interests, which made Susie immensely proud, but I also began to see jealousy develop in her. Heather was exceptionally talented as an artist and was creative in the dramatic arts. Susie prided herself in all these things, and she would constantly compare herself with her oldest daughter. In many ways, Heather had the same personality as Susie but without the mental illness. This did not help their relationship. Katie began to show a great deal of talent in singing and acting as well as playing a drum set. Susie took a lot of pride in her own natural rhythmic skill on the drums, but as Katie surpassed her ability, Susie began to form some jealousy with her as well. Katie developed her musical and dramatic talents, of which we were both proud, but it was somewhat problematic for Susie. I'm sure the girls both felt this tension, but they fortunately did not suppress their drive to grow in the artistic talents the Lord had given them. All of this began to show me the childlikeness that Susie seemed to have in all her relationships.

One time a dear friend of Heather's who was an owner of an antique store had passed away in her home. This was crushing for Heather; she had grown close to this older woman and had wonderful conversations with her over the years. We very much wanted to support Heather in this difficult time, although we did not fully understand how close she had become with this woman. For Heather it was like losing a parent. I know as I look back that I would have been much more understanding of Heather's grief had I realized how close she had been with this older woman. In many ways she had been a replacement for a mother, since Susie was not able to fill that role adequately. I now regret not being more aware of that, but we parents can all look back and see where we went wrong. Fortunately, God covers our mistakes more than we realize.

We were invited to come to the funeral of this dear woman. Heather even was asked to speak. She had been known by many people in the community, and the attendance at the funeral reflected the affection people had for her. During the service, Susie began to cry almost uncontrollably. I leaned over trying to calm her but also was surprised that she was taking the death of this woman so hard because we barely knew her. After a bit I asked Susie why she was so upset. She said she was afraid there would not be nearly as many people at her own funeral. I was a bit taken aback that at a time when we were there to honor someone else and at the least to support our daughter in her grief, Susie would be so emotionally upset over concern for herself. The self-centeredness of this really bothered me although I did not tell Susie that at the time. It only reinforced the childlikeness that I began to see more and more in Susie's outlook on everything.

As I have mentioned before, Susie would often blame either her mother or me for her struggles. After her mother passed away, I became the sole target of her blame. I know that I certainly added to some of her struggles with my own baggage. I was learning how to deal with someone with mental health issues and often did and said the wrong things. I'm sure I did not appreciate her enough or tell her how beautiful she was enough or show enough affection at times. All that said, she would often complain about our marriage and say that we should never have gotten married in the first place. I was not tall enough, wealthy enough, strong and manly enough, or just was not what she had wanted. It was hard to hear these things, but down deep I knew much of this was coming from a place of insecurity and deep unhappiness with herself. Because of her feelings, I dreaded going to anyone's wedding when invited. I knew that after going I would hear all her unhappiness with me, and that could trigger an episode. She would come home and be furious with me because I wasn't affectionate enough or romantic enough or the husband I should be.

After one of those weddings, she lost all hope in a future that could contain happiness, and she took a knife and cut her wrists in an attempt at taking her life. Whether this was a serious attempt or not, I could not say. She did not cut nearly deep enough into her wrists to have killed her, but it was enough for us to have her hospitalized once again. She spent a week in the hospital as the doctors adjusted her medications, and she got some needed respite from normal responsibilities. As an example of how all of us had become a bit numb to the life of one drama after another with Susie, Kate, who was now in college, recalls being angry when she heard the news about the latest suicide attempt. In her mind it was just another self-centered act on her mother's part. We all were becoming a bit hard-hearted, I guess, but I believe it was just a survival mechanism. When Susie came home from the hospital, she and I went for some marriage counseling, which lasted for a couple sessions before it became clear to the doctor that she needed separate and individual sessions. Again, I say this not because I was such a great husband but because her issues needed more immediate attention. In hindsight I can see how I made so many mistakes in our relationship but also realize that I was not able to make her happy. While I wanted to please her, I was not the one responsible for her happiness. It was her own responsibility, and she certainly was having a difficult time being happy with any consistency. One of the counselors we had seen made a life-changing observation in our relationship that helped me a great deal. He told me that I was not able to be her counselor *and* her husband. I needed to concentrate on just being her husband. That was easier said than done because I constantly needed to give her pep talks and remind her of her value to me and her daughters and of her own self-worth. I eventually got better at it.

Chapter Twelve

Leading Worship during a Long Period of Struggle

I WANT TO TAKE SOME TIME TO EXPLAIN MORE ON HOW THIS ALL AFFECTED ME professionally. As a full-time worship director/pastor I still needed to lead worship every Sunday, even when I was at some of my lowest points in life. Being the transparent person I am, I was not trying to hide my struggle. I think I survived by compartmentalizing my life into professional/worship leader and personal/husband and father. I had no idea if I was doing the healthiest thing, but I found it necessary to keep my sanity. I suppose some could look at my life at that time and think I was play acting at one or the other. I would speak very positively and worshipfully when I was up front on Sunday mornings or with the people at church, and I would try to be the same at home but was much less positive. Some may call this hypocrisy, but I was only doing what I needed to do to survive. What saved me from being called a hypocrite during this time was that I was not hiding the fact that I was in the middle of a difficult struggle and needed prayer and support. I was very transparent. I remember one time that I started a worship set during a Sunday service by saying I did not feel like singing that morning. I did not even feel a lot of love for the Lord that day. I even felt a bit angry at God. I explained that it had been a particularly rough week, and it was not much better on that morning. After I had finished sharing where I was at emotionally that morning, I explained that others may feel the same way, but God does not expect us to worship because we feel like it. We worship God because He is worthy of all our praise and all our worship. His love for us has not changed. He is still good. He is still in control. We can still trust Him. "Now," I said, "let's worship." I am amazed to this day how people still come up to me and tell me how much that Sunday meant to them. I was just being myself and sharing my heart on that day with the congregation and offering myself to God to use me even in the state of mind I was in. He was faithful. He used me even when I was not feeling in a good place with Him.

There were times, however, that I was too transparent with too many people. I remember one Sunday morning I began to share a bit of helplessness I was feeling, and I began to cry … from the platform. You may be saying, "It's okay for a man to cry in public. There is nothing wrong with that." I would agree with you, but this went a little overboard. I completely lost it. I mean I was blubbering. I made a lot of people uncomfortable, including myself after the fact. People became overly concerned about me and wondered if I was falling apart. I had begun to reassure people that I was doing okay and that I just lost control for a moment and in a very public way. I would never advise anyone doing that. When people love you and look to you for leadership, it is better to break down with just the few people that you are closest with who will know you are just unloading the emotional stress that has been building up. Fortunately, people in the church loved me, and it was soon forgotten.

I cannot emphasize enough how much some close friends played a part in keeping me sane and able to persevere. These few people knew just about *everything* Susie and I were going through and stayed by us and went through it with us. These people were God-sent, and I will always appreciate their love and support. I don't believe it is healthy for anyone to go through extremely difficult times alone, especially if they extend over a long period of time without some close friends to talk to. In each of the churches I worked during the years we dealt with Susie's mental health, there were friends who knew about it and were there for us. God never wants us to live our lives isolated and alone. He has placed us in families. These *family members* are sometimes blood and sometimes just close friends who pray and listen and support us in many ways.

I also must share that I was constantly trying to be a good father who was offering support and a positive outlook on life for two daughters going through the normal stress that preteens/teenagers go through. Sometimes I was exceptionally good at it and other times failed miserably, but God was again faithful and gave both of my girls an ability to go through all of this with strength and grace. I am so proud of the women they have become and the heart they have for people who struggle. God poured out His grace on our family when we needed it most.

I heard an illustration today in a sermon of God's faithfulness through struggles that touched me.

> The early American Indians had a unique practice of training young braves. On the night of a boy's thirteenth birthday, after learning hunting, scouting, and fishing skills, he was put to one final test. He was placed in a dense forest to spend the entire night alone. Until then, he had never been away from the security of the family and the tribe. But on this night, he was blindfolded and taken several miles away. When he took off the blindfold, he was in the middle of a thick woods and he was terrified! Every time a twig snapped, he visualized a wild animal ready to

pounce. After what seemed like an eternity, dawn broke and the first rays of sunlight entered the interior of the forest. Looking around, the boy saw flowers, trees, and the outline of the path. Then, to his utter astonishment, he beheld the figure of a man standing just a few feet away, armed with a bow and arrow. It was his father. He had been there all night long. (Soul Salsa, Zondervan 2000, pg 23-24, Leonard Sweets)

God allows us to go through difficult times but never leaves us alone. It is in these times that we grow and learn how to deal with life and the struggles that come with just being a part of this fallen world. He is our Father and will *never leave us or forsake us.*

CHAPTER THIRTEEN

Hearing from God?

As we continued our life in Minnesota, our family experienced all the normal things people go through. Our girls were now teenagers in high school and were heavily involved in theater and speech. This came as no surprise to either Susie or me since we were so heavily involved in the arts as well. We had tried to encourage our daughters in other, more financially lucrative directions but to no avail.  Susie and I enjoyed going to all their performances and competitions and frequently had their friends at the house. Most of their friends simply loved Susie with her unconventional personality and humor. They would call her Mama Zehr and joke around with her. Susie loved this time of the girls' lives and always spoke so favorably about the times she was able to spend with our daughters and their friends. I must say as well that we enjoyed every stage of growth our girls went through. Every stage, that is, except the last year of Heather's high school days. Heather and Susie fought a great deal, and they would exchange words that were hurtful. Heather was very anxious to get out of the house and be on her own and wasted no time after her graduation in moving out.

As with so many young people, Heather had to experience life and learn lessons on her own. She began to hang out with people that caused us great concern. Heather began to live a life of moving about from house to house and sleeping on friends' sofas. She traveled with this community and lived the life of circus people, never staying long in one place. She soon became involved with a guy who did not go by his true name but by a name he made for himself that described his personality and the way he wanted the others in his community to view him. Soon Heather moved in with him. Susie and I were concerned, as we knew he was about seventeen years older than her. I did some digging to try to find out his real name and even tried to do a background check on him because the situation looked so suspicious and dangerous. Fortunately, he turned out to not have any kind of criminal background. Remembering that makes me laugh a bit at the thought that I would go to such measures, but she was, after all, my baby girl, and I felt very protective of her. They lived in a communal house with people coming in and out all the time. This made our concerns for Heather even greater. We were afraid of losing our daughter and tried hard to stay engaged in her life. At one point we prepared a Thanksgiving dinner for everyone at their house because we wanted to show our love and acceptance of them and just to get to know them better. The communal house was not an exceptionally clean place with all sorts of people going in and out, with some living there and others camping in the back yard. At one point Susie decided to stay the night at the house to reconnect with Heather. I know this was hard for her with her OCD. She slept on the couch with cats running around, and people up throughout the night. I will always look back on that event, however, and admire the lengths she would go to show love for her family. It was a tremendous sacrifice she made but Heather was worth it to Susie. She would also go to Heather's drum circle events and participate. It was clear that Susie and Heather were now reconnecting and even forming a special bond. They had so much in common with the same interests and love of laughter. Heather invited Susie to join her face painting, performing, and basically being involved in many of the fun things Heather was doing. I think they understood each other in a way I probably never could. Susie was living with the tension of loving many of the things Heather was involved with artistically but concerned about some of the other aspects of the path she had chosen to walk.

Susie would think it was all her fault that Heather left the house so early and got involved with the subculture she did. I would always try to reassure her that our children make their own choices in life regardless of how we did as parents. We both admitted to making many mistakes in our parenting, but I felt we could not go down the path of guilt and regret. Susie would listen but continue to blame herself and her inability to be the mother she wanted to be. She was very accustomed to blaming herself for everything and lived with tremendous guilt even about things over which she had no control. This, I believe, was something she learned at a young age from her mother. Susie never really learned some of the tools that most of us take for granted that help us to deal with the normal struggles in life. She had an extremely poor self-image and was very childlike in her approach to relationships and dealing with life.

This insecurity drove her to try so hard to hear from God in a supernatural way. Just hearing encouraging words from me or friends was not enough. She wanted to hear from God Himself, either as a voice or specific Bible scriptures to know beyond a shadow of a doubt that He loved her and was proud of her. At times she would tell me that God spoke to her and told her to do something that was obviously not a divine message.

Once Susie felt God told her to make a cake, though she was not a good baker, and that He was going to give her the step-by-step instructions without a recipe. She followed what she believed was God's instruction and finished this chocolate cake. She felt so proud of it and was anxious for me to try it. When I got home, she told me all about her day and cut a piece of her cake, placed it on a plate and set it before me. I was a bit cautious because I knew that Susie had no idea how to make a cake from scratch, but she was so excited. I picked up my fork, cut a bite off, and put it into my mouth. She looked at me anxiously and said, "Well, what do you think?" I smiled a crooked smile and told her politely that it was … okay. She wondered what I was talking about and promptly took a piece herself. After tasting a bite, she said, "Oh, this is awful!," and threw it away. We both laughed at how horrible the cake tasted. However, it made Susie feel like she was an idiot to think God would talk to her. After all He didn't really love her anyway. After a long conversation, she accepted the fact that she may have heard wrong and that it was not at all a reflection of God's love for her.

Susie continued to try to hear God's voice in ways that really concerned me. Once she felt absolutely certain God was telling her that He was going to give her the gift of flight. If she would just trust Him enough, He would allow her to fly like a bird. She went out and stood in the middle of the backyard, put her arms out and faced heavenward, and waited for God's gift to show up. I felt extremely sad when she told me about this experience that day, picturing her standing out there waiting for God to show her how much He loved her by giving her the ability to fly around the yard. In many ways it reminded me of a story she would tell me about her biological father saying he was coming to visit her. She would put on her nicest dress and sit on the living room couch for several hours waiting. But he never showed up. The thought of her going to such extreme measures believing she heard from God made me concerned. I was so grateful she did not go up on the roof and jump off expecting flight to begin. I decided to take her to another doctor and have her evaluated again.

This doctor told us that she had another disorder in addition to OCD, Tourette's, and bipolar depression. Susie was also now suffering from schizo effective disorder. This is like schizophrenia but not quite as severe. Susie was now hearing voices in addition to having intrusive thoughts. The thoughts were dramatic enough, but now voices were telling her things, and they were louder than the thoughts. With this diagnosis, she was put on additional medication and began a specific type of group counseling that was rather intensive and lasted a full year. We were both getting rather exasperated at all these diagnoses and getting frustrated. She was now seeing a psychiatrist, a therapist, and a special therapist for the OCD. This amounted to three doctor's visits per week, none of which she could get to on her own since her driving was so poor. That left me to take her as much as I possibly could and a friend to take her when I could not.

The OCD therapist would work with Susie to try to face the fears that came in the form of intrusive thoughts and in the facing of them, dispel them. This all sounded good and logical until one day Susie took it a little too far. One of the intrusive thoughts was that she wanted to take a knife and stab me in the stomach. This was just one of the thoughts that urged her to hurt me, our children, or our beloved pet dog. Since the doctor had told her to face the fear of stabbing me in the stomach, Susie went to the kitchen and picked up a large knife. Now that was as far as the therapist wanted her to go with the exercise, but Susie misunderstood. I was lying down on the couch in the living room reading a book when Susie walked in with the knife and told me what her therapist had told her to do. I thought that was very strange and, of course, told her I felt uncomfortable with it. She began to say things like, "You really think I could act on these voices, don't you? It really is me. I'm a terrible person!" She said this because she was always looking to me to reassure her that the thoughts and voices were not her at her core but that it was her illness. I told her I knew she did not want to hurt me. She wanted me to let her put the knife to my stomach but nothing more. As uncomfortable as I was with her doing that, I knew that she would never hurt me and that down deep she loved me too much. I let her put the knife to my stomach for just a few seconds and then promptly told her that was enough. She felt that down deep I was afraid that she would stab me and that I was trying to hide the fact that I thought she really was a horrible person. I reassured her that she was not but that I thought she had misunderstood her therapist. I went with her to the next appointment she had with this doctor and was reassured that indeed she never meant that Susie should do that. I never put myself in that position again. From that point on I never trusted that Susie was hearing correctly from her counselors and almost always went in with her to hear what the therapists and doctors were telling her.

CHAPTER FOURTEEN

Childlikeness

AFTER SEVEN YEARS HAD PASSED SINCE OUR MOVE FROM FLORIDA TO Minnesota, the church where I was working that had called me to join the staff asked me to resign. This was mostly due to a difference in vision between the pastor and me. The hardest part about this was not that I was asked to resign but that in November I was asked to stay on until Easter and not tell anyone that I would be leaving. This meant staying silent and acting as if nothing had changed for a period of about five months. I understood this was to keep unity in the church and not cause a split, which is often the case in many churches. I was able to do that but not easily. This was particularly hard on Susie. She was not a person to keep quiet about her own pains and struggles and found it difficult not to tell her friends. She became rather bitter and angry at the church in general. For her this was the last straw after seeing how I had been treated at previous churches as we went through what we now called the "worship wars." It had been many years of hearing how I wasn't doing things correctly and that hymns and the organ were the true forms of worship. Not only was my spirituality and faith questioned but my character as well.

It was extremely hard on my family to see this husband and father criticized so fiercely.

The church, however, was exceedingly kind and gave me six months' severance pay while I searched for a different job. This was not an easy time for Susie as she saw me trying to find work and even doing some house painting to help us stay afloat. She was a woman who desperately needed security, and having a husband without a full-time job made her especially insecure and scared.

It was no coincidence, however, that the day I started my next job at a different church was the day my severance pay from the previous church ended. God is good. Unfortunately, I had to take a rather drastic cut in pay ($20,000 per year), and the church was a thirty-minute drive from my home, causing my expenses to go up. It was a wonderful church, smaller than the one I had left with the average age considerably older. These factors, combined with her hurt from churches as a whole, left Susie not wanting to be a part of my new church. She felt guilty at not being the wife she thought she was expected to be but just could not make herself attend on any kind of regular basis. She also continued to fight panic attacks, particularly in crowds, and struggled with them every time she attended church. We also found ourselves in a much more difficult financial place due to the cut in pay and eventually had to declare bankruptcy. All these stresses together, along with her mental and physical struggles, began to take their toll on Susie. She became worse in her mental health and even more childlike in her approach to me and her life.

I say even more childlike because that was a definite characteristic of Susie over most of our marriage and even with some of her time as a mother. I remember once Susie had decided to have a "play hooky" day with the girls when they were younger. They were in elementary school at the time. She pulled them out of school and took them to see a movie. While I really didn't have much objection to that, seeing that it was a good mother-daughter bonding time, I did object to what she did when the movie ended. She asked the girls if they wanted to see another movie. When they said they did, she proceeded to show them how they could just pop into another theater before anyone saw them and find a seat to watch another movie for free. When she came home and told me what she did, she couldn't understand why I thought that it was not a good thing to have done and that it was like teaching the girls it was okay to steal a movie. She thought I was just being a killjoy and brushed me off. The girls, of course, felt the same as their mom because they had had such a good time together. It wasn't that what they did was so terrible in and of itself but that their mother was teaching them something that went against my personal moral code.

Another time Susie had taken the girls to the mall for some shopping. She was in that same kind of mode of wanting to have fun with the girls, so she decided to do something with them that was a bit *edgy*, particularly for an adult. She decided to show the girls how much fun it was to throw spitballs at unsuspecting people and watch their reactions. From the upper level of the mall she began throwing spitballs down on the people on the floor below. I was not there, but I can just image them laughing and having a fun time watching the people below. One man who was passing below looked up, noticed what they were doing, and said to Susie, "What is wrong with you!" For some reason even that did not sink in with her and give her pause. All these incidents demonstrated to me how childlike she was in her mind. If it was fun and not hurting anyone, it was perfectly okay to do.

I suppose it was the fact that she was so childlike in her approach to life that showed itself as selfishness to me. She could never really think about the consequences of her actions but rather if that action was fun or was beneficial to her. So many times she seemed to be totally unaware of the needs of others or was completely out of touch with the things they were going through at any given time. One of the people in our lives that Susie referred to as her best friend found herself in some difficult circumstances. She was working at a job that was putting heavy amounts of stress on her and working for a man who was an extremely difficult person to work with. Not only that, but her husband had been diagnosed with bladder cancer and was undergoing some rather difficult treatments for the illness. Susie was aware of all that was happening in her life but never really showed any concern for her. In fact, one day she surprised her by showing up at her door with a big smile on her face. "Hi," she said. "How ya doing today?" Her friend replied she was having a bit of a rough day. "Why?" Susie said as if she should be happy because Susie was having a good day. She rarely took anyone else's situation into account and approached life from a very self-centered point of view. Whether this was because of her illnesses or something she learned from a mentally ill mother who approached life in that same way or not I do not know. Often when my birthday or Christmas came around, Susie would ask a mutual friend what I would like because she genuinely did not know what I would enjoy as a gift. Our relationship was simply about meeting her wants and needs, and mine came a very distant second.

Later, Susie was given an additional diagnosis that now included borderline personality disorder. This is a disorder related to bipolar but is not treated with medication but rather through intense therapy. I discovered over the course of her therapy that this disorder came about through the many different traumas in her childhood. This explained why in so many ways she remained a child in her approach to life and the way she dealt with difficulties and even relationships in general. I began to be more of a father figure to her rather than a husband as I took care of her every need. She began to see me that way as well and even teased me that I was like her dad. She also felt as if our good friend was like a mother to her, as she would pick up the slack that I could not handle. One time I was extra busy directing a cast of forty people in a community theater production and had invited Susie to sit in on rehearsal. I was pulled in many, many directions answering questions from all sorts of people when Susie came up to me and said in a childlike voice, "I'm hungry and need to eat now." She was totally unaware of my immediate situation. All she knew was she was hungry, and I was the one who could relieve that hunger. This reminded me of how our daughters would do this same thing when they were young.

Soon after that, I felt like a wall came between us relationally, and I began seeing her more as a daughter who needed to be cared for rather than as a mate. She also became less and less the woman I married who was full of life and fun and spunk. Her face began to show signs of weariness, and the spark was completely out of her eyes. She began to forget where she was and became less and less steady on her feet. While her mood swings were gone, she still was totally unsure of herself, scared and crying all the time. At this time I was glad I had a thirty-minute commute to and from the church. When I got off work, I would call her to tell her I was leaving and on my way. I did this not only to let her know of my status but also to give me an idea of what kind of mood she would be in when I got home so I could prepare to deal with it.

We would find ourselves in the same room every night watching television without saying much of anything to each other. She was simply not able to carry on a conversation with me or any of her friends. Any responsibility was overwhelming for her. We had a puppy, which we both loved, but Susie found it overwhelming to take care of him and asked a friend if she could take him. The friend had to remind her that the dog was not just hers but mine as well, and she needed to consider what I wanted too. This became the norm for Susie. She simply could not think of anyone but herself. I'm sure this mostly had to do with her illness, but also it was a sign of how childlike she had become.

As we approached our thirty-fifth wedding anniversary, I felt strongly that we needed to celebrate it big and take a trip to the United Kingdom and specifically Ireland and England as these were Susie's countries of origin. We could not afford it, and we were uncertain if Susie could handle the crowds and walking and so forth. We decided to do it anyway and really celebrate thirty-five years together. It was a wonderful trip, and I am so glad we did it even though it was obvious in the pictures we took that Susie was only half there. Little did I know that this would be the last trip we would take together.

CHAPTER FIFTEEN

Susie's Last Weeks

SUSIE'S HEALTH SEEMED TO BE DETERIORATING. IT WAS NO LONGER ONLY HER mental health but her physical health. She was no longer walking with any endurance and seemed to be stumbling and falling much more than normal. She no longer had any spark in her eyes and face and had almost completely lost her sense of humor. She had a history of pneumonia, so when she got a cold, we usually went to the doctor right away to make sure we got ahead of it.

In late February 2018, I had gotten a nasty cold that lasted almost a week. We were both concerned that Susie would catch it but were pleased when after almost a week she was showing no signs of the illness. Later that week, however, she began to show signs of a cold. We waited to go to the doctor because it really did not seem like it was progressing. After a couple days, however, she seemed to be coughing rather deeply. We went to the doctor to make sure things were not moving toward bronchitis or pneumonia. They took x-rays and did a thorough examination, and it was determined that it was a bad cold. Due to her history, however, the doctor gave her an antibiotic and told her to pay attention to everything and get lots of rest. Susie was not a healthy person at the time and because of her OCD she was always afraid she was dying, so both Heather and I felt like things were not as bad as she was making them out to be. A few days later she did not seem to be getting any better, so we went back to the doctor to get her examined. Once again, the doctor examined her and said there was no sign of bronchitis or pneumonia and sent us home. Heather came over to be with us and to comfort Susie particularly during the next day, which was Sunday, and I would need to be at the church. Sunday morning, after a call from Heather, I returned from the church service. Heather told me that her mom was not doing any better and that in fact she was having a hard time walking to the bathroom. After a couple of hours, it was clear something was not right, and she needed to go to the emergency room at the local hospital. I called an ambulance because she was getting to the place she could not walk, and I could not carry her down the steps and out the door on my own. The paramedics came and had a special chair they used to get her into the ambulance. Heather and I followed them and got her admitted right away. After a few hours in the emergency room and more x-rays it was determined that she had developed pneumonia in the last day or two. The staff even showed us the difference in the x-rays that clearly now showed pneumonia, which had not been there three days before. They then checked her into the hospital and later into the ICU.

It was now day thirty in the ICU with Susie being hooked up to a respirator to breathe. She had been admitted with pneumonia that now had progressed to ARDS (adult respiratory distress syndrome). It was a month that took an emotional toll on all three of us. One day we would feel optimistic about her getting off the machine and improving. My Facebook friends can attest to that roller coaster ride with every post I would put up. One day we were encouraged, and I would make mental plans as to where Susie should go next for therapy, and the next day, I would be making mental plans as to how I was going to make it in life on my own. I had even called Kate home from Chicago because I thought her mom was on her last few days. After Kate had been there a full week, it appeared Susie was rallying, so she went back to her home in Chicago. Heather continued to visit almost every day to support me and to be there for her mother. Susie continued to get worse. Every time we would try to extubate her, she went into a panic, and the doctors would have to flood her with antianxiety medications and reintubate her. Finally, we all agreed it was coming to the end of the struggle. I had called both of my girls to come and join me in the ICU as it began to seem that there were not many days left for her. They came with their significant others and began the heart-wrenching process of trying to determine how long to let this go on and if we should take Susie off the respirator. One doctor had suggested that we could still wean her off the machines, and then she could go into a special facility to gain her strength back through about a year's worth of therapy. For her to get off the ventilator meant that Susie would have to handle being off sedation. It was the only way she could go to the facility to get weaned off the respirator. Each time the doctors would reduce her sedation, all the machines would alarm as her body would begin to panic. I knew Susie simply did not have the will to do what she would need to do for that treatment. She had an advanced directive stating she did not want to be kept alive on a ventilator in any way that would leave her in a coma state. This was one of her greatest fears, and she had made me aware of this on countless occasions. It was a torturous time as I tried to determine what to do. I felt that I had the responsibility of determining whether Susie lived or died. It was horrible. I was so pleased when, finally, one of the ICU nurses pulled me aside and told me that she was surprised that Susie was still in ICU and that she did not give her much hope of ever being extubated. I know this was a somewhat risky thing for the nurse to do, as she had to be careful not to cross a professional line with this kind of advice. I was so relieved to hear her words and almost felt they were divinely inspired because that was also my feeling, but I was afraid to give up on her. When we finally told the doctor of our decision to let Susie go, the doctor said he agreed.

It was the hardest thirty minutes of my life, and the lives of my oldest daughter, Heather, and her wonderful husband, Pat, and my younger daughter, Kate, and her wonderful boyfriend, Elohim, to watch the life slowly disappear from Susie's body. I was so grateful that I had my good friend and pastor there to support me. We all just sat there holding her hands, with me singing to her the song she heard me sing when we first met. It was the song that Susie said caused her to fall in love with me: "Turn Your Eyes upon Jesus." We began to see the color go out of her skin and her lips turn gray. I can barely even type these words right now as my eyes fill with tears. It was an extremely painful time for us all and particularly painful when her heart stopped beating, and we took her off all the machines. I knew that Susie would not be able to be there when her daughter got married in four months and that she would never get to meet her grandchildren. I knew, however, that she was finally dancing with Jesus with freedom and an expression that was filled with confidence in God's deep love for her. I knew that maybe for the first time Susie was certain of God's incredible love for her. I was rejoicing for her, but at the same time it did not ease my pain, as I would not have her with me anymore. I would now have to learn to live alone and start a whole new life.

We began to make plans for a memorial service to celebrate Susie's life and how God used her in our lives. I felt so incredibly supported as we began to put the service together. A dear friend with whom I had worked in Florida was able to fly up from New Mexico and sing. Another dear friend of Susie's from Florida who knew her for many years before we were married was able to send a letter to be read in the service. Another dear, close friend of both Susie and mine who had been there through all the rough times shared her thoughts and feelings as well. Both girls found it within themselves to share some exceedingly difficult but wonderful memories of their dear mother and include the song "Hey Jude" by the Beatles in the service, which they had sung frequently with Susie. I had been a choir director at each church where I worked, and Susie had often helped me find songs for the choir to sing that would be powerful testimonies of God's faithfulness. I had asked if possibly a few of the choir members from my previous church in Minnesota and my current church could combine and sing one of her favorites. I was absolutely overwhelmed to see how many members came to be a part of this combined choir. I was extremely touched. What was probably the most meaningful thing of all, however, was to see the number of people who attended the April memorial service in a surprise blizzard. It was one of the worst blizzards I had seen in Minnesota in the seventeen years we lived there. Even so, the church was packed. I couldn't believe it! Family from Wisconsin, Illinois, Arizona and Missouri came. People from both churches in Minnesota came. The sanctuary was packed with people supporting the girls and me as we celebrated Susie's life—and through a major April blizzard! The girls and I said it was just their mother's characteristic to go out in a big way. Strangely enough, we have had a blizzard every April since her passing. I guess she doesn't want us to forget her.

Life with Susie had extreme ups and downs. I married the most beautiful and talented woman I have ever met. She used to make my life complete. Yes, I had many, many difficult years of trying to make her happy and meet her needs, but I knew we were meant to be together. God had made it clear that we were perfect for each other. I needed her vitality and life to make me come out of my German shell, if I had one, and really enjoy life to the fullest. She needed my caretaker nature to help her through life's difficulties. I am not the man I was when we got married. I have learned to be more understanding and tolerant of people who are different than me and know that if they are harsh or unkind it is probably because of some difficulty in their life of which I am not aware. More than anything, however, I have learned that Christ truly can be "closer than a brother," and while He never promised to keep us from strife and difficult times, He did promise to never leave us and to be there with us through those times. I will forever be grateful to Susie and the Lord for allowing me to be a part of her life and to help her through it. The book of James says, "Consider it pure joy, my brothers and sisters, whenever you face trials of many kinds, because you know that the testing of your faith produces perseverance. Let perseverance finish its work so that you may be mature and complete, not lacking anything" (James 1:2–4 NIV).

EPILOGUE

LIFE AFTER SUSIE HAS BEEN A MAJOR ADJUSTMENT FOR HEATHER AND KATE AND me. A week after her memorial service was her birthday, which was not an easy one for us. Then came Mother's Day a few weeks later followed by our wedding anniversary a few weeks after that.

Next came Heather's wedding, which took place a couple months later. It was a bittersweet experience as we celebrated the union of a perfect couple. Susie so loved her new son-in-law-to be, Pat, and was anxious for him to be an official part of our family. It was a beautiful wedding—a true celebration. I was so happy that Heather wanted to have a peacock theme to the wedding, which was Susie's favorite bird. They also had a special memorial table with pictures of Susie with the girls and me. It was a wonderful tribute to her mom and I am so glad Susie was made a part of her daughters wedding. It was beautiful to have Susie's memory present even though it was still not the same as her being there. It obviously was an emotional day for us all.

We have all tried to live our lives as best we could knowing that Susie was no longer with us. The girls and I made a special effort to get together a year after her passing just to reminisce and place flowers at her gravesite. We continue to go through life grieving at our own pace and staying as close as ever. God continues to be close to me and proves to be a support and guide as I try to find and develop a new life on my own.

James tells us that we will go through various trials and struggles but that we are to count it all joy. Some may say there is no way that

God actually means to count struggles as a joy. I believe He means exactly what He says. I heard an illustration in a sermon the other day that speaks very well to this point.

> Once a little girl found a cocoon hanging from a limb in the forest. She took it to her room and placed it in a jar, expecting one day to see a butterfly emerge. One day, she saw the butterfly within the cocoon trying get out. It was struggling and trying to push its way out of the tight opening. To help the poor insect, she very carefully slit open the cocoon. Soon after, the butterfly was able to easily exit the cocoon. But a strange thing happened. Instead of spreading two beautiful wings, the butterfly had two withered, shriveled, useless, ugly wings hanging by its side. Why? God designed the butterfly and his cocoon so that the tight opening would straighten and strengthen his wings. Without the pressure of the tight opening, the butterfly was robbed of the beauty of his wings, and more importantly, he was robbed of the ability to fly into the heavens. He was condemned to a life of walking around on the ground!
>
> (sermoncentral.com, "Strength in Weakness," Chris Layton)

If we are committed to trusting God to always have our best interests at heart, we can trust Him to know why He is allowing us to go through things that seem like they are only harmful to us and can only cause pain. We must remember He is our Father and loves us far more than we can understand. He loves us more than we love our own children. If we only want what is best for our own, how much more can we trust He has our best interest in mind.

Over the years many people have asked me how they can hear

from God or have said they wished they could hear from God like I have. I have to say first and foremost that there is absolutely nothing special about me. Believe me, if you knew me you would agree. In fact, I believe that many people hear from God daily and just don't realize it is the Holy Spirit leading and guiding them and giving them wisdom for each moment of their day. Sometimes He has spoken to me in rather loud and dramatic ways but much more often it is in very subtle and quiet ways that I could easily have missed if I had I not been looking and listening for it.

I have also seen God speak to me so many times through music. Whether it was through a worship song or even a secular song, I have felt I heard God speak a truth in a way that I could receive it and remember it. Music is a powerful tool for either good or bad, I suppose. The music itself, without lyrics, can break down our defenses and open out hearts to receive a message. When lyrics are involved, they pierce your soul to reach a part of you that is usually guarded and protected. God has used both sung and instrumental music in my life over and over to speak to the deepest parts of me and minister to hurts and wounds in a way I cannot explain. I am grateful for that gift in my life.

I have been learning and studying scripture almost my whole life. From a young age I have been in Sunday school classes, attended vacation Bible school, and participated in family devotions. I have been through many scripture memorization programs and done a lot of Bible reading and study on my own. Nothing I ever heard from God went against scripture; in fact, most words I felt I received from God were actual scripture. I remember Susie would oftentimes struggle, saying she could never hear from God. She would open the Bible, close her eyes, and point to a verse in scripture believing that God would supernaturally direct her to a verse she needed to hear. Does God ever work this way? I'm quite sure He does, but that is not the way He has worked with me. I remember times when I felt very strongly that the Lord was confirming a decision to move or make a big decision through the scripture I was reading at the time. Could I have misinterpreted His voice? Absolutely! But God knows my mind and my tendencies to hear things. While I know I have misunderstood the signs or the scripture on more than one occasion, most of time it showed itself to be spot on, particularly when bounced off a respected friend or relative.

My constant prayer is: *Lord, You know how I can mess up hearing what You have to say, so just weed out whatever it may be that is not from You.* I have made it a habit to read the Bible daily, not for the purpose of getting an answer to a specific problem but more to learn more about the character of God and His overall revelation to mankind. When I take that approach, I find I am more likely to hear correctly. When I was younger, I would use the topical index of a Bible looking for a specific promise that would apply to whatever I was going through at the time. It was at those times that I usually misinterpreted His voice. The Bible can be an answer book to specific problems, but more it can be seen as God's love letter to us to reveal His heart and mind. Don't get me wrong, I have gone days, even months, without reading the Bible. It was either times when I was mad at God or was going through an extreme dry spell in my spiritual life. I remember a dear friend telling me once not to feel guilty about those times. We all go through them. In those times we can withdraw from our spiritual savings accounts to get us through. We may not be making any deposits right now, but we are living off years of earlier deposits. I took a lot of comfort in that statement.

I also spent many years of memorizing scripture either through rote memorization methods or through songs. As an actor (or at least a wanna-be actor) I was able to memorize rather quickly. I say I *was* able to because now I'm at an age where it is not nearly as easy. I even once memorized the entire book of James and recited it in a Sunday church service. It was a great experience that I would never be able to do now. I have greatly benefited, however, from those years, and I still pull on those words from James constantly in my life.

We have such a great and awesome tool in the Bible as God's revelation to us. The Bible even speaks to itself when it says, "All scripture is God-breathed and is useful for teaching, rebuking, correcting and training in righteousness" (2 Timothy 3:16). When we immerse ourselves in the Bible, we open our minds and hearts to hear from God on a regular basis. It is also a great way to check any word we feel we are receiving from God. If it does not align with scripture, you can be certain it is not from God. I would often go to people I loved and respected spiritually and bounce the word off them. Many times, I would find myself so deeply wanting to hear a specific word from God that I would think I heard just what I wanted to hear rather than what God intended for me. These trusted people would be able to see that and lovingly steer me in the right direction. That is one advantage to living in a community of believers that love you enough to tell you the truth.

All that being said, hearing from God is not a science. If hearing correctly from a spouse or other person in your life is something that must be learned and practiced, how much more is hearing correctly from God, who is not here in the flesh with us. It takes practice and an open heart willing to admit you can make mistakes. My ability to hear from God or not is not what determines my self-worth or my worth in the eyes of people. It certainly has nothing to do with how much God values me. I have known people who seem to think that they are "important" because they are getting special revelations from God. Our ability to hear from God is not a litmus test on our spiritual walk or our importance to the community of believers or the world. God created us all with great value as children of His, and our worth is rooted in that fact alone, not in what we can do or not do. Know you are immeasurably important to God and loved by Him simply because you are a creation of His. His understanding of your life and His love for you goes far beyond our own understanding.

If I had to sum up any advice to people who may have a loved one that struggles with mental illness or knows someone who is trying to be a caretaker for someone struggling with mental illness it would consist of these four things: draw close to God, really listen to the person without giving advice and love that person, find a support group, and, finally, remember that life here is but a fleeting moment and that we live for eternity.

First, truly draw near to God. When we cry out to God, He has promised to hear us and never leave us. The scripture says, "Come near to me and he will come near to you" (James 4:8). Prayer is not just an exercise to help us feel better but an actual conversation with the One who knows and loves us and can give us everything we need to persevere. He will also give you the ability to see your loved one through His eyes. This may mean seeing the person the way he or she *will* be instead of the way he or she is right now—the way God meant for the person to be had he or she not had the life he or she had or been afflicted with this illness.

Second, learn to truly listen to the person you are caring for. So many times, we want to give answers to people's problems to help them get through their struggles when what they really need is just for someone to listen and be there for them. Go on the journey with them. I remember so many times people with good intentions wanted to tell me what they thought the problem was and what I needed to do to fix it. We as Christians are particularly guilty of this because we feel we should have the answer. Some of the most helpful people in my struggle were the ones who were just there and willing to go through the struggle with me rather than give me a prescription for making things better.

Third, find a group of people you can trust who are willing to go through the journey with you. I say a group of people because you do not want to put an emotional burden of this size on any one or two people. Take advantage of several people who can help carry the day-to-day responsibilities as well as those who can walk with you through the emotional ups and downs over a long period of time. Some people are only able to be there for you once or twice. Be grateful for those people as well, but look for friends or family that will be there for you over the long haul.

Finally, the person going through the difficult time may feel that it is unending with no relief in sight. The scripture says, however, that God "has set eternity in the human heart" (Ecclesiastes 3:11). We live our lives on this earth with the goal of a heavenly home. I know, for me, when I took on this perspective I was able to persevere through what seemed to be an endless tunnel with no light at the other end. One of my lifelong favorite verses is found in Isaiah 40:29–31, which speaks to a hope that only comes from the Lord.

> He gives strength to the weary and increases the power of the weak. Even youths grow tired and young men stumble and fall; but those who hope in the Lord will renew their strength. They will soar on wings like eagles; they will run and not grow weary, they will walk and not be faint.

Sometimes I think we look for fun and happy feelings so much that we lose sight of being what God meant us to be. That is not to say that this life should not be filled with joys and wonderful experiences, but our purpose on this earth is not necessarily to feel happy but to do good and put others before ourselves. This can give meaning to our lives that surpasses any pursuit of fun and happy feelings. We put our hope truly in the Lord knowing that the fulfillment of that promise in Isaiah may not be experienced here on earth, although we certainly hope it will. We know that eventually we will receive that reward when we face Jesus in eternity. That being said, we can still find incredible joys here on earth just by putting others before ourselves and seeking deep, meaningful things. That meaning and purpose can and does give deep joy and peace and, yes, happiness.

I am so grateful that God knows every detail of my life. My every thought and feeling is known and understood by Him. I find a great deal of comfort knowing that even though He knows all the thoughts in my mind and heart, He still has a love for me that is wider than the ocean and deeper than the sea, as it says in the song Wider that the Ocean by Dennis Jernnigan. As the scripture says, "I pray that you, being rooted and established in love, may have power, together with all the Lord's holy people, to grasp how wide and long and high and deep is the love of Christ, and to know this love that surpasses knowledge—that you may be filled to the measure of all the fullness of God" (Ephesians 3:17b–19 NIV).

ACKNOWLEDGEMENTS

I WANT TO SAY A SINCERE THANK YOU TO SOME SPECIAL FRIENDS WHO HAVE helped me in the writing of this book. They have both encouraged me and supported me as I endeavored to do something that was a stretch for me both emotionally as well as physically in the actual writing.

Thanks to Blake and Laura who, as writers, encouraged me to tell this "compelling" story and gave me editorial advise before submitting it to a publisher. Thanks, also, to my dear friend Liz who was not only my friend but Susie's as well and helped me remember specifics that aided in describing the feelings and emotions we all felt at different times.

Of course I would be remiss if I did not say thank my wonderful daughters who gave me their permission and approval to tell this story. While their versions would be a bit different they respect that this was my perspective on all that took place in those many years. I am exceedingly proud of both of them and the wonderful young women they have become.

I would also like to thank the many people, both friends and family, who have loved and supported my family through all of the struggle and trials. At all four of the churches where I worked I found people who stood by us and loved us in as many ways as they could. Without their constant support I doubt I would have been able to make it and continue leading worship through it all.

Obviously, the greatest thanks goes to the Lord who made me and stood by me everyday and night through those many long days of loneliness and despair. He truly is a friend that is closer than a brother.